D0324189

Faces in the Crowd

B.J. HOFF

Celebrating Our God
Who Knows Us By Heart

Faces in the Crowd

B.J. HOFF

Celebrating Our God Who Knows Us By Heart

Artwork by
JUDY HAND

WARNER Press

Design by Dianne Deckert
Calligraphy by Christine McGucken
Edited by Cindy Maddox

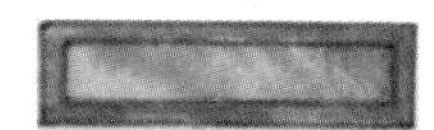

AUTHOR'S ACKNOWLEDGMENT

Any author is blessed to work with the kind of people who make up Warner Press. They truly have been a gift of God to me.

Faces in the Crowd represents the efforts and dedication of too many to name, but please know that I'm deeply grateful to all of you. There is no measuring the contribution of your hard work, your encouragement, and your prayers.

My special thanks to Cindy Maddox, Administrator of Product Editors at Warner Press, who gives so much of herself to make sure that what I do is the best it can be.

ISBN: 0-87162-650-0 Stock # D7521
Printed in the United States of America
Warner Press, Inc.

DEDICATION

O MY READERS:

This book is dedicated to you, friends. We share many common experiences on this journey called Life: the changes and challenges, the struggles and successes, the trials and triumphs.

We also share the most glorious heritage imaginable, for we are children of one Father, one Creator, one God. Whether you have known God for years or only a day . . . whether you acknowledge His sovereignty and name Him as Lord or are just taking the first steps in your search for the Truth . . . one fact is common to us all: He loves us.

In our crowded world, amidst all the rush and confusion, the trouble and turmoil, we need more than ever to realize that each one of us is known . . . known and remembered and cherished. Each of us is unique . . . and uniquely loved. Our God's love is so all-encompassing, so unconditional, that He comes to each of us where we are, no matter where we may have been or what we might have done. He comes with open arms and a forgiving heart.

Every promise God has given us reflects the love of a Father for His own: *"I have engraved you on the palms of my hands."* The cross is the ultimate proof of that love: *"This is how we know what love is: Jesus Christ laid down his life for us."*

This book is to reassure you . . . and myself . . . that we are not merely "faces in the crowd" to our Father-God. We are His creation, His children, His beloved. I hope you will consider it a gift to you, with my heartfelt thanks, for your letters, your encouragement, and your prayers.

"Grace and peace to you from God
our Father and the Lord Jesus Christ."

B. J. Hoff

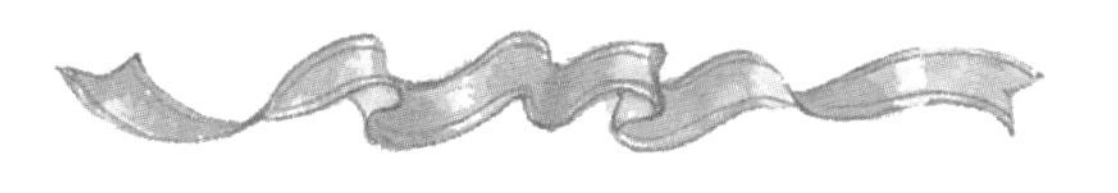

Faces in the Crowd

TABLE OF CONTENTS

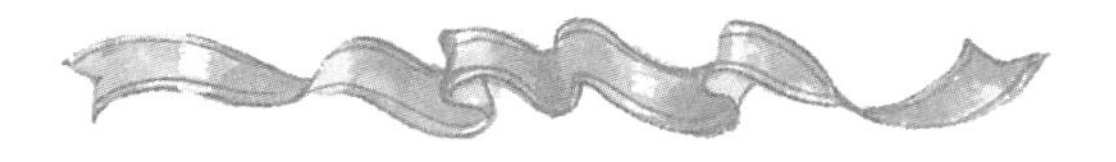

CROSSROADS

VALLEY OF SHADOWS

MOUNTAINTOP MOMENTS

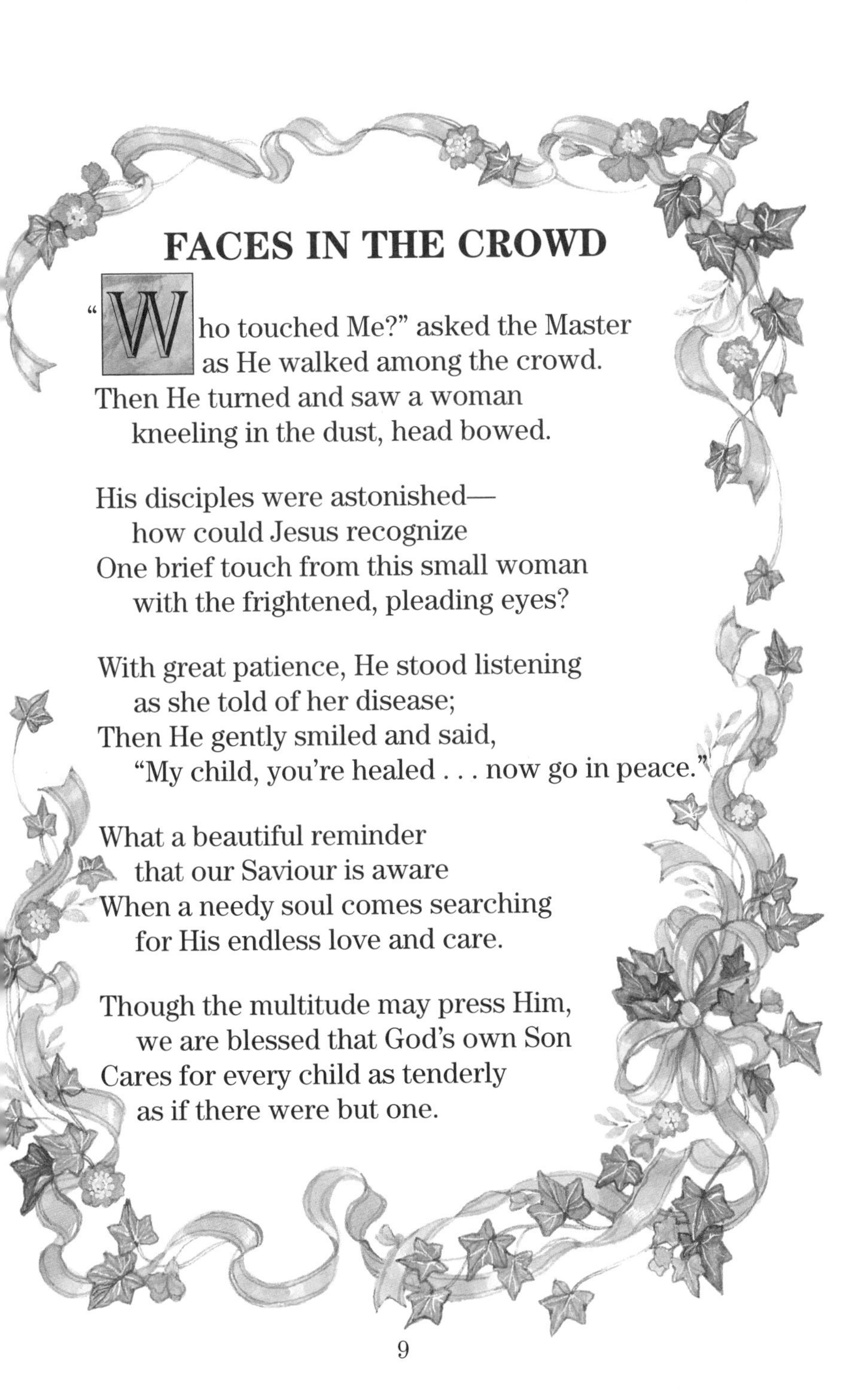

FACES IN THE CROWD

"Who touched Me?" asked the Master
as He walked among the crowd.
Then He turned and saw a woman
kneeling in the dust, head bowed.

His disciples were astonished—
how could Jesus recognize
One brief touch from this small woman
with the frightened, pleading eyes?

With great patience, He stood listening
as she told of her disease;
Then He gently smiled and said,
"My child, you're healed . . . now go in peace."

What a beautiful reminder
that our Saviour is aware
When a needy soul comes searching
for His endless love and care.

Though the multitude may press Him,
we are blessed that God's own Son
Cares for every child as tenderly
as if there were but one.

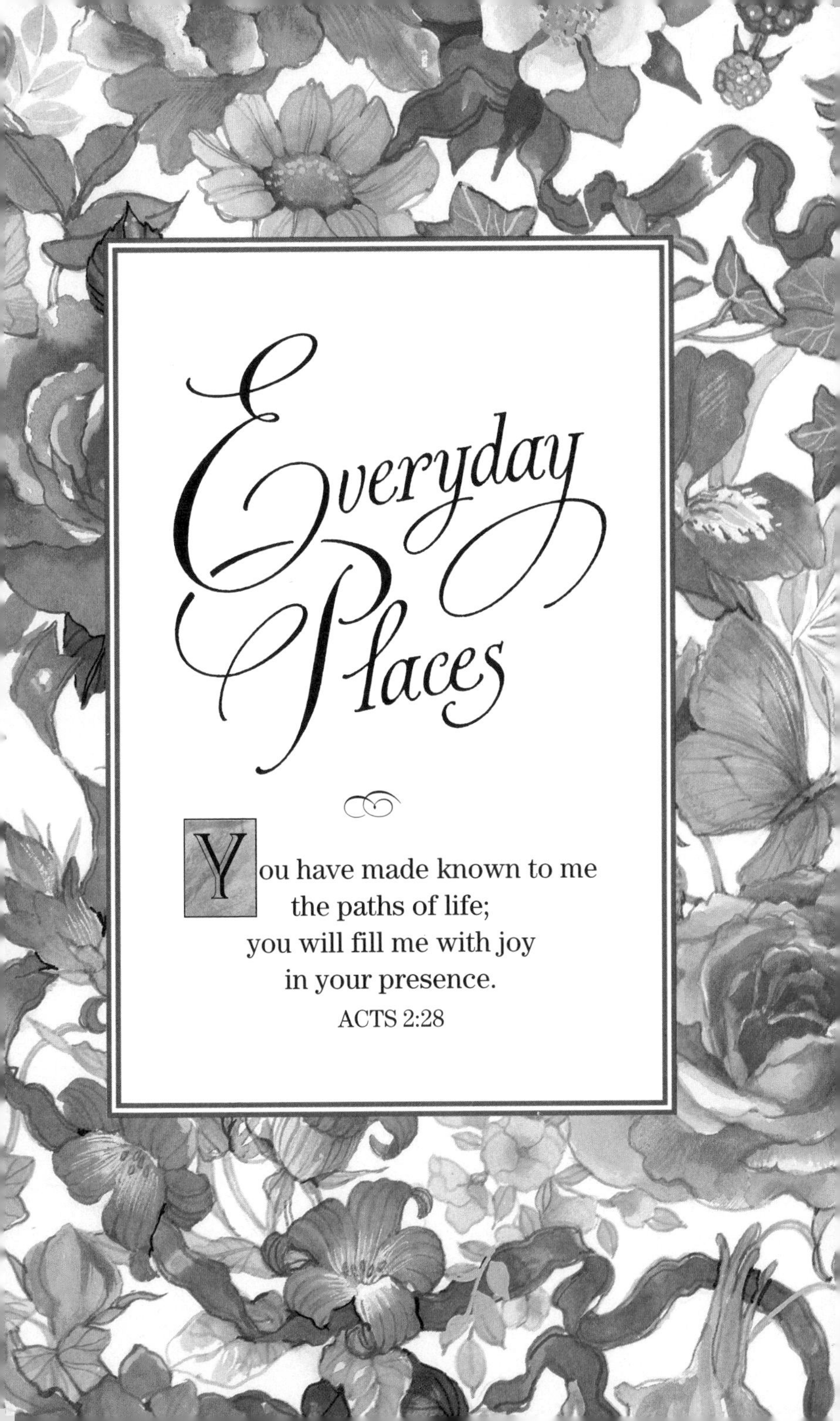

Everyday Places

You have made known to me
the paths of life;
you will fill me with joy
in your presence.
ACTS 2:28

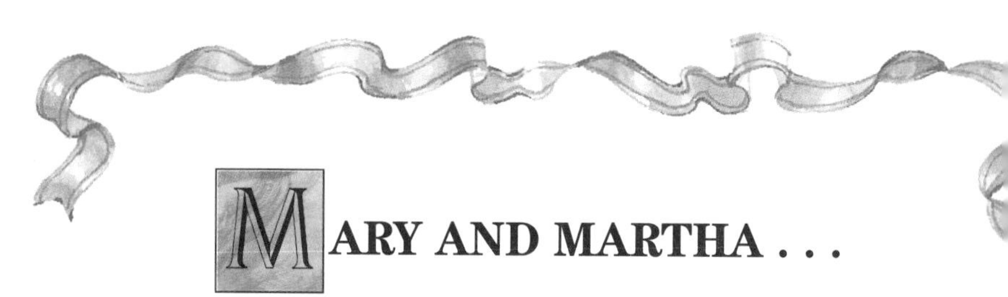

MARY AND MARTHA . . .

THE BETTER WAY

But Martha was distracted by all the preparations that had to be made. She came to him and asked, "Lord, don't you care that my sister has left me to do the work by myself? Tell her to help me!"

"Martha, Martha," the Lord answered, "you are worried and upset about many things, but only one thing is needed. Mary has chosen what is better, and it will not be taken away from her."

LUKE 10:40-42

Martha bids Jesus welcome,
flings wide the door
and greets Him warmly,
then turns away
and races for the kitchen
to prepare a feast
fit for the King of kings . . .
while Mary kneels before Him
in the threshold dust
to wash His feet.

Up to her elbows in flour,
kneading bread,
Martha lends half an ear
to the Master's words.

But Mary, hungry for other things,
sits quietly consuming
the Bread of Life.

Martha works and frets and throws herself
into doing the things that need done.
Planning, preparing, performing,
she chooses to do,
to act, to accomplish.
At last, weary with doing,
she lashes out at idle Mary,
who still sits at the Saviour's feet.

But Mary has chosen a different way,
a better way, the Master says.

Martha serves with distraction,
labors under the strain of self-sacrifice,
obeys with a heart of resentment
and garnishes her offering with bitterness.

Mary gives only herself:
a quiet soul,
a listening love,
a heart of adoration.

Nothing is more important to her
than fellowship with Jesus.
She chooses the better way,
and her hunger is satisfied.

THE ADVENTURE

We ask God to reveal His plan,
His purpose for our lives,
But turn our eyes upon a distant hill.
We clutch our dreams, as if they're woven
From the dust of heaven,
Convinced that they reflect the Father's will.

We fix our goals, committed
To great things that will live on,
Achievements that will glorify God's name,
Unwilling to acknowledge
The desire that lurks within,
That what we do might also bring acclaim.

We look ahead, beyond today,
To see where God may lead—
There's always one more mountain to ascend.
We hurry through our days
As if the future might not wait,
As if all that really counts is Journey's End.

But God's intent for us
Is never anchored in tomorrow,
His purpose is for here and now . . . today.
God wants this life to be
A grand adventure, not a blueprint.
Our part is just to trust Him and obey.

We glorify God best
By taking one step at a time.
We please Him most by living every hour
In constant celebration
Of His never-failing love
And in absolute dependence on His power.

For we fulfill God's purpose
And delight His heart as well
When we walk the journey with Him, hand-in-hand,
Discovering that His presence
Makes each moment something precious—
And we're living the adventure that He planned.

Trust in the Lord and do good; dwell in the land and enjoy safe pasture. Delight yourself in the Lord and he will give you the desires of your heart.

PSALM 37:3, 4

LORD OF MY LIFE . . .

Be my daily guide upon the journey. . . .
Help me find Your purpose for my life
in the everyday.
Let me catch a glimpse of Your glory
in the commonplace.
Make me wise enough to treasure
the here and now
As I trust the future to You.

TAKE NOTHING FOR GRANTED

Lord, enable us to live
With thankful hearts at every moment,
Mindful of our blessings, big and small. . . .
May we never take for granted
Your abundant gifts of goodness,
But continually be grateful for them all.

Better one handful with tranquillity
than two handfuls with toil
and chasing after the wind.

ECCLESIASTES 4:6

GIVER OF ALL GIFTS . . .

For every dear, familiar face in my life,
every smile, every touch, every grace . . .
For every gift of the day, no matter how commonplace
or small it may appear . . .
For every blessing of beauty, every moment of peace,
every goodness in which I can rejoice . . .
I give You thanks with every breath I take.

GENTLE GUEST

His coming was quiet—
no clash of cymbals,
no blast of trumpets—
just the midnight song of angels
and the awe-filled sighs of shepherds
on a hillside hushed by holiness.

His coming is still quiet—
His call is tender,
His pleading soft—
just a whisper of love in the silence
and a gentle touch of promise
to the humble heart that bids Him welcome.

I stand at the door
and knock.
If anyone hears my voice
and opens the door,
I will go in and eat with him,
and he with me.

REVELATION 3:20

KING OF MY HEART . . .

How many times have You come to me,
amidst the noise and clamor of my life,
only to be passed by or ignored?
How many times have I longed
for the peace of Your presence,
the light of Your wisdom,
the comfort of Your love,
when all the while You've been there,
standing by, waiting for me
to come away from the crowd
and commune with You?
Gentle Saviour, give me a quiet heart . . .
always open to Your coming,
ever sensitive to Your whisper,
quick and eager to welcome You
with gladness and rejoicing.

CELEBRATE THE MOMENT

Look around . . . take in this moment,
it will never come again.
Accept the blessing, feel its warm embrace.
Glimpse the glory of the Giver
in the wonders near at hand.
Celebrate, for God is in this time and place.

Light is sweet,
and it pleases the eyes to see the sun.
However many years a man may live,
let him enjoy them all.

ECCLESIASTES 11:7, 8

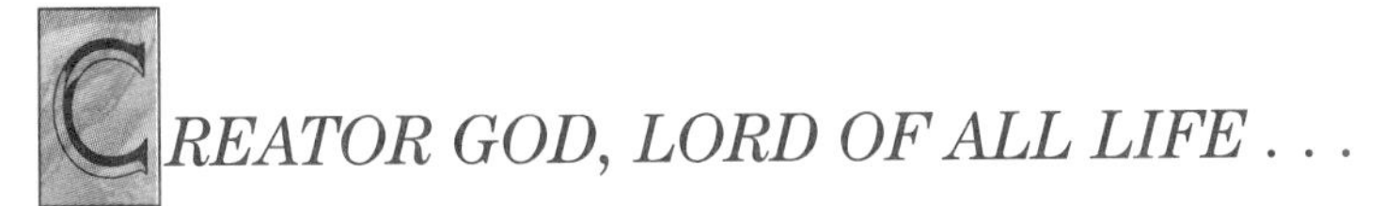

CREATOR GOD, LORD OF ALL LIFE . . .

Teach me how to cherish every moment of my life . . .
To recognize the blessing and the gift
of the present,
instead of racing through my days
on the way to the future . . .
To realize that on this day . . .
in this hour . . .
at this moment . . .
I am in the presence of the King.

PLACE OF ABIDING

I bring to You
my hopes, my plans, my dreams
for Your safekeeping,
trusting You to do with them
whatever You think best. . . .

I wait on You in perfect peace,
my faith securely anchored,
my soul rejoicing in Your love,
my anxious heart at rest.

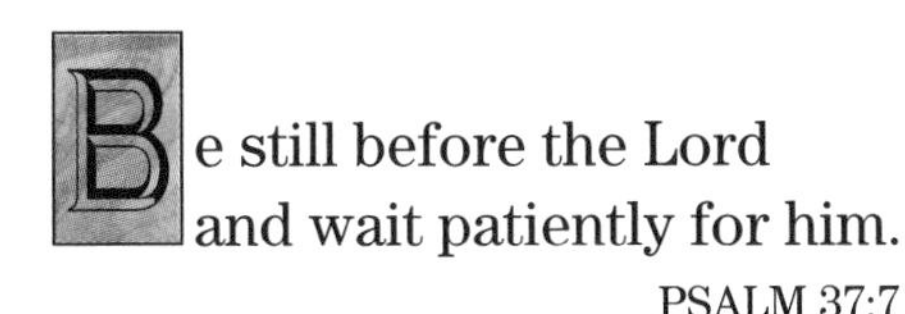

Be still before the Lord
and wait patiently for him.

PSALM 37:7

I have stilled and quieted my soul; . . .
like a weaned child is my soul within me.

PSALM 131:2

GUARDIAN OF MY SOUL, MY FAITHFUL REFUGE . . .

The shelter of Your love, Lord,
  is my haven.
Freed from the struggle
  of trying to fulfill my own dreams
  and order my own life,
I can rest in Your arms
  and be at peace.

AFFIRMATION

It matters not
if the world has heard
or approves or understands. . . .
The only applause
we're meant to seek
is that of nail-scarred hands.

Well done, good and faithful servant!
You have been faithful with a few things;
I will put you in charge of many things.
Come and share your master's happiness!

MATTHEW 25:21

DIVINE MASTER . . .

To You, who left Your heavenly throne
to come as a helpless Baby . . .
To You, who exchanged Your kingdom's crown
for a wounding wreath of thorns . . .
To You, who received scorn instead of acclaim,
whose worldly reward was the shame
of the cross . . .
To You, and only You, do I come seeking
the affirmation, "Well done, faithful servant . . .
well done."

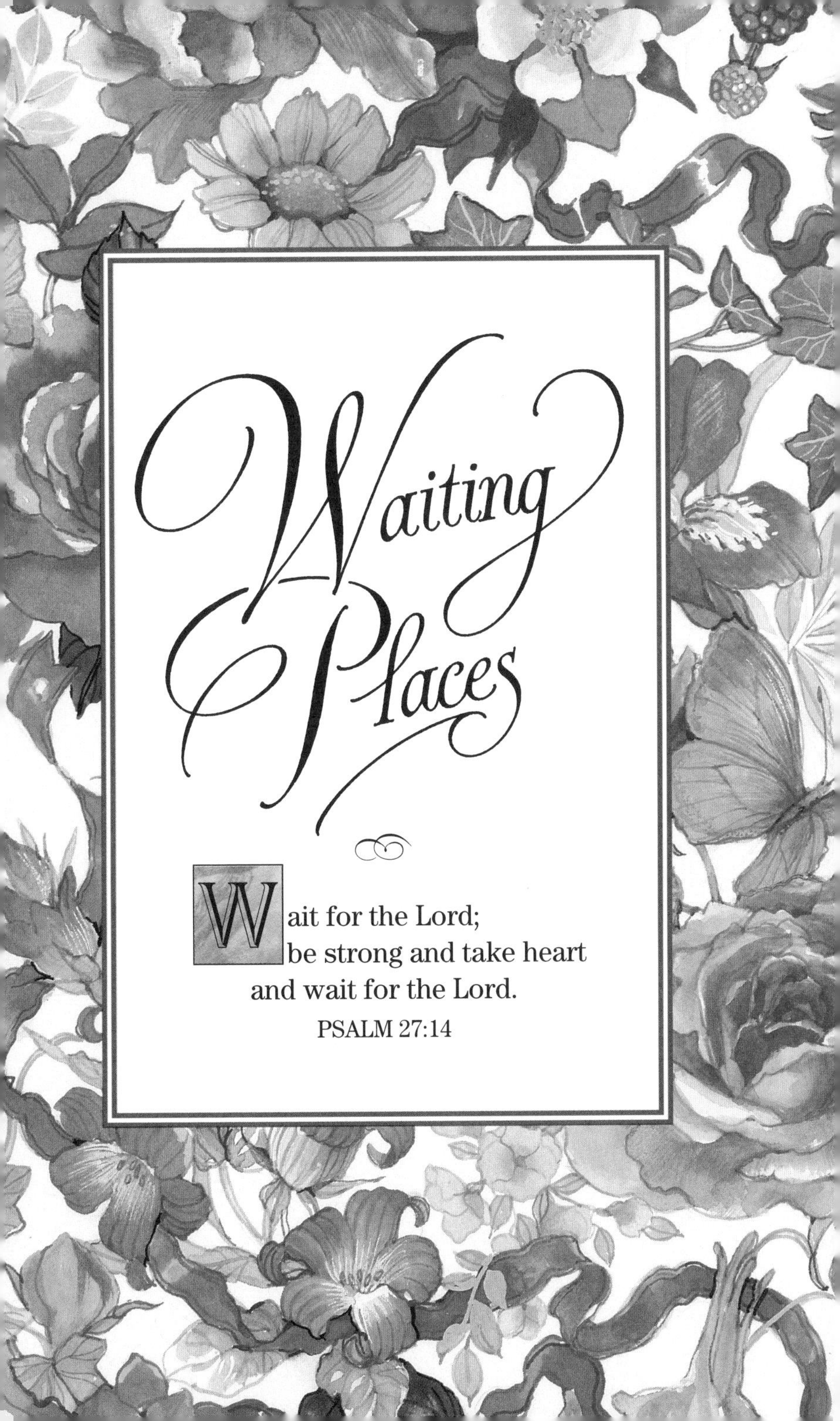

Waiting Places

Wait for the Lord;
be strong and take heart
and wait for the Lord.

PSALM 27:14

ANNA . . .

A STEADFAST HOPE

There was also a prophetess, Anna . . . . She was very old; she had lived with her husband seven years after her marriage, and then was a widow until she was eighty-four. She never left the temple but worshiped night and day, fasting and praying. Coming up to them at that very moment, she gave thanks to God and spoke about the child. . . .

LUKE 2:36-38

For eighty years and more,
she lived and served within the temple.
From bride to widow, girl to woman,
she watched the seasons of her life unfold and flow.
Time spread its web across her face
and drove the fruitful days of youth
to a secret place within.

She chose to wear the years with grace,
busy with becoming.
Her quiet ways
wove gentle harmonies into her song of solitude.

Alone, but not bereft,
she learned that thought and prayer and work
make good companions.

Throughout the years,
her woman's heart was healed,
her faith fulfilled and strengthened.
Nurtured by hope, her spirit thrived,
grew rich and deep and fertile.
Yet, something in her soul seemed poised,
as if in waiting.

Then, drawn to the sound of Simeon
praising in the temple,
Anna found him with an infant in his arms.
A childlike mother hovered near,
clutching the sleeve of her husband,
as the two of them gazed with wondering eyes
at Simeon and their Son.

Moved by the Spirit's touch, Anna approached
to glimpse the Babe—
and felt the sun explode inside her soul!
The song came thundering like a wave,
the *Gloria* swelled and trembled
as the waiting place, the empty space
in her heart was filled at last.

DETOURS

Life's journey includes detours—
changed plans, failed dreams,
wrong-way turns, even dead-ends.
Sometimes we feel abandoned,
left to wander in the wilderness
of defeat, discouragement, and despair.
But in His time, God steps in
to give Direction.

We often chafe when we're forced
to retreat or stand still and wait—
we want to advance.
But God knows we need training
and faith-building
and lessons in trust . . .
Discipline.

We strive to achieve, but God says, Learn.
We strain to run, but God says, Walk.
We struggle to do, but God says, Be . . .
And trust Me
with your Destination.

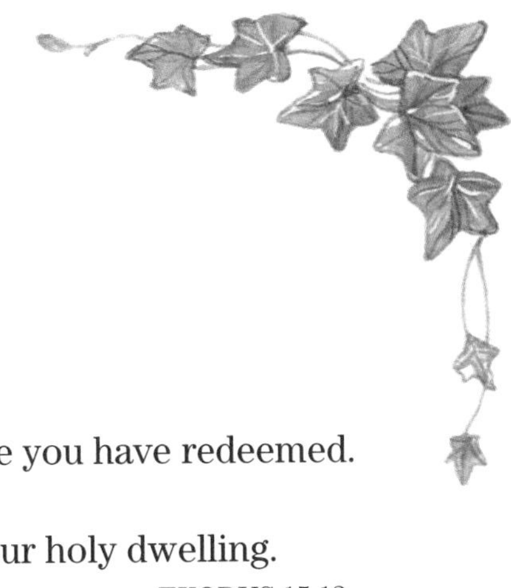

In your unfailing love
you will lead the people you have redeemed.
In your strength
you will guide them to your holy dwelling.

EXODUS 15:13

MY GOD AND MY GUIDE . . .

Light my every step upon life's journey. . . .
Whether I'm walking or standing still,
changing courses or pressing straight ahead,
may I live every moment close to You, in Your love.

LIGHT AND SHADOW

When it seems
as though my prayers
are simply bouncing off the walls,
When doubt dims my faith
like shadows in the night,
Help me look beyond the problems
of the moment to Your power;
Help me trust You
in the darkness or the light.

Let him who walks in the dark,
who has no light,
trust in the name of the Lord
and rely on his God.

ISAIAH 50:10

Now faith is being sure of what we hope for
and certain of what we do not see.

HEBREWS 11:1

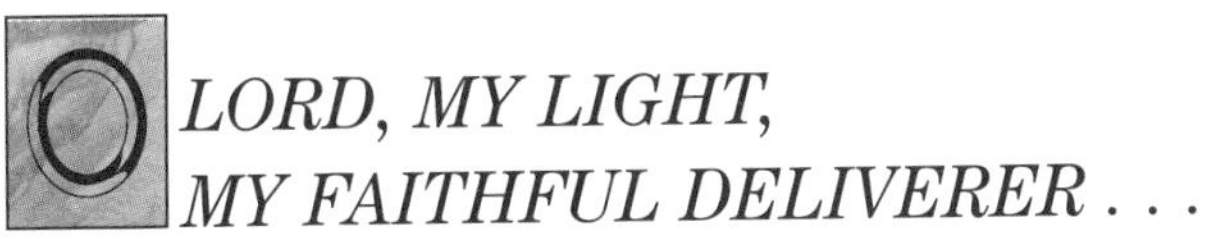

O LORD, MY LIGHT,
MY FAITHFUL DELIVERER . . .

Let me learn to view my problems
from the perspective of Your power . . .
Looking to Your light in my darkness,
Your love in my loneliness,
Your strength in my weakness.
You have never failed me, Lord,
and I know You never will.

WHEN THERE ARE NO ANSWERS

Life will bring us questions without answers.
To live is to encounter silent seasons of the soul,
When every prayer will seem to go unanswered
As we face events beyond our understanding or control.

Yet in the quiet darkness, Christ is working.
His silence in the shadows doesn't mean He doesn't care—
A part of faith is trusting without reason,
Believing, when He can't be seen or heard, that He's still there.

So when answers fail to come, don't be discouraged.
Keep leaning on God's steadfast love and trusting in His will,
For knowing *why* won't really make a difference—
But growing close and knowing Jesus *will*.

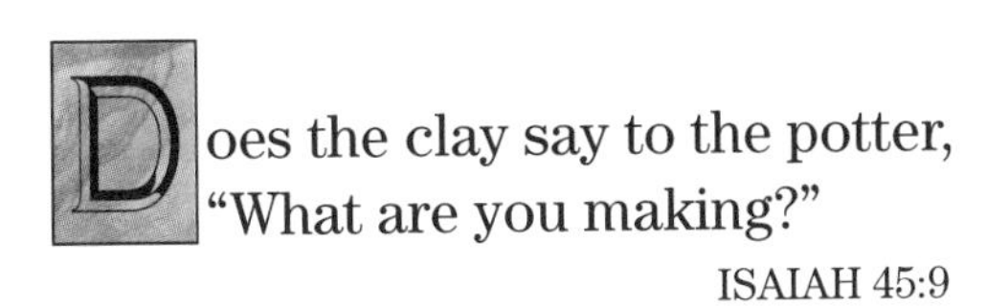

Does the clay say to the potter,
"What are you making?"

ISAIAH 45:9

Trust in the Lord with all your heart
and lean not on your own understanding.

PROVERBS 3:5

MERCIFUL AND SOVEREIGN LORD . . .

Teach me to be still and rest in You.
Give me, Lord, a faith
that doesn't depend on reasons or answers
or constant reassurances of Your love . . .
a steadfast faith that stands on Your Word
and trusts in Your goodness,
knowing there is never a moment
when I'm out of Your care.

PURPOSE FOR MY LIFE

Oh, Lord, I'm feeling old today—
Used-up, spent, and in the way.
I'm feeling sorry for myself,
As though my life were on the shelf,
With nothing new to celebrate,
Nothing to anticipate,
No one to pass the hours with me,
No plans to make, nowhere to be.
The loneliness is crowding in
Like hammer blows of pain again.

In vain I seek to fill the hole
Of heartache deep inside my soul.
I call up long-forgotten things—
Old memories, hopes, and faded dreams.
But nothing from the past can ease
The emptiness or bring me peace.
Only You, Lord, can replace
This barrenness with warmth and grace.
Only love—Your love—can give
Fresh meaning to each day I live.

Teach me to delight my heart
In all of life, each precious part.
Let me treasure quiet days,
Living them in constant praise,
Reassured I'm not alone,
But loved and cherished as Your own.
Keep me close, and help me find
The purpose which Your love designed
For all my days, till this life ends
And Everlasting Life begins.

What does the Lord your God ask of you
but to fear the Lord your God,
to walk in all his ways,
to love him, to serve the Lord your God
with all your heart and with all your soul,
and to observe the Lord's commands and decrees?

DEUTERONOMY 10:12, 13

LORD OF MY LIFE,
MY TODAYS AND TOMORROWS . . .

Deliver me from the snare of self-pity.
Remind me that, when I'm unable to work,
I can pray . . . I can praise . . . I can *be*.
The cross makes me worthy.
Your love makes me whole.
I am cherished and precious in Your sight.

A QUIET WAITING

Strength is often found
within the silence,
while resting in the presence
of the Lord.
Abiding in God's peace,
we feel His power;
while leaning on His love,
we are restored.

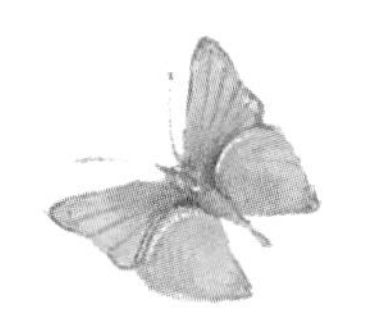

But [the Lord] said to me, "My grace is sufficient for you, for my power is made perfect in weakness."

. . . That is why, for Christ's sake, I delight in weaknesses, in insults, in hardships, in persecutions, in difficulties.

For when I am weak, then I am strong.

2 CORINTHIANS 12:9, 10

LORD, MY STRENGTH,
MY ROCK OF REFUGE . . .

Help me to abide in You,
casting all my cares on You,
resting as I lean on You
and trusting in Your love.

LIVING IN THE LIGHT

Longing for Your light, I search,
eager, expectant, impatient to get on,
to go forward, to grow,
convinced that even one gem of revelation
from the vast treasury of Your wisdom
would shine like the sun in my soul,
would take me where I want to go
on this journey of the spirit.

Then You pierce my stubborn seeking,
break my resolve, revealing the truth
that light comes not through demands
or study or yearning,
but by one small step of obedience.
Only then do I find myself
walking in Your light,
closer to Your heart than ever before.

Oh, the depth of the riches of the wisdom and knowledge of God!
How unsearchable his judgments,
and his paths beyond tracing out!

ROMANS 11:33

Those who obey his commands
live in him, and he in them.

1 JOHN 3:24

LIGHT OF THE WORLD,
LORD OF MY LIFE . . .

Keep me walking in Your light,
following Your truth, obeying Your Word . . .
not worrying about what I do or what I am
or where I'm going.
Make me willing to walk, or to wait,
whatever Your call.

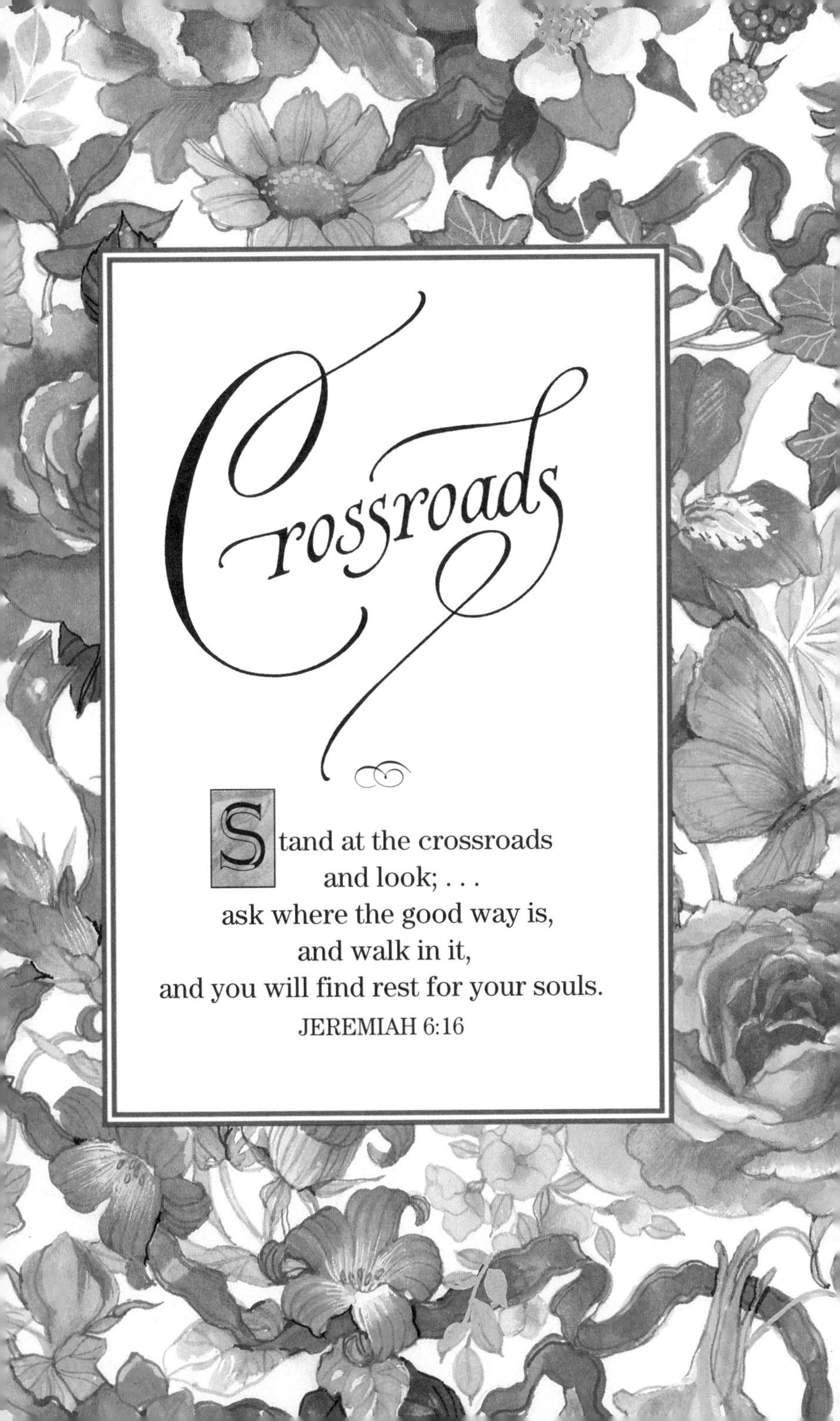

Crossroads

Stand at the crossroads
and look; . . .
ask where the good way is,
and walk in it,
and you will find rest for your souls.

JEREMIAH 6:16

JOSEPH . . .
A FAITH FOR ALL SEASONS

"So then, it was not you who sent me here, but God."

GENESIS 45:8

Beloved son, indulged and favored,
Joseph proudly wore his coat of many colors,
sign of his father's love.
He dreamed of glory, saw himself standing tall
as his brothers knelt before him,
and he told them of his dream.

His immaturity and pride cost him everything:
his brothers stripped him of his plumage,
that cherished symbol of belonging,
and cast him, bewildered and trembling,
into a deep dry well to await the slavers
who would take him into Egypt, the Dread Unknown.

Enslaved in a foreign land, Joseph laid down his pride,
became a trusted servant, honored, true,
bearing the keys of the household
as symbol of his master's faith.
The Dread Unknown became his home.

But his master's wife betrayed him
with poisoned words and vicious lies,
stripped him of his trust, and cast him into prison,

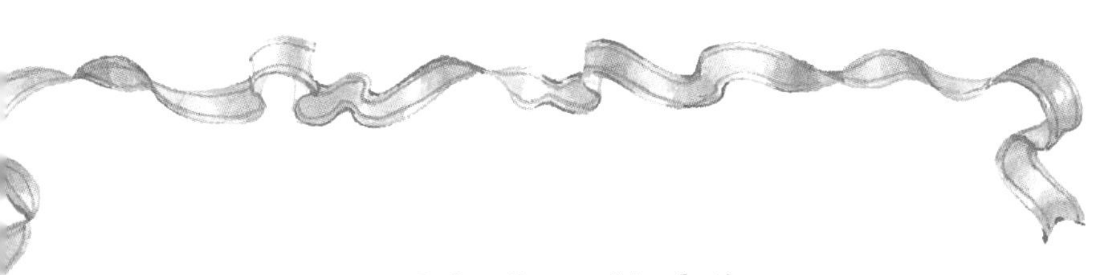

where solitude and the fires of isolation
forged his faith.
He wasted no energy on anger or despair,
but proved himself faithful in his duties,
sweeping his cell as if it were a holy call,
honoring his God in the darkness of the dungeon.

At last, his faithfulness in little things
raised him from the pit to sit beside the king.
Joseph's dream came true:
his brothers knelt before him where he stood,
with the glory of Egypt thrown over his shoulders
like a mantle of many hues.

But his solitary days of holding to his hope,
clinging to his God, had changed the man within.
Molded by pain and loneliness,
he grew in wisdom and faithfulness.

They had taken his robe, but not his integrity . . .
his family, but not his fidelity . . .
his wealth, but not God's opportunity.

For the Lord was with Joseph, in prison and palace,
in an empty well, in a dungeon cell,
transforming pride into humility,
self-confidence into loyalty.
Through it all, God was with him, fashioning a man
fit to wear the many colors of his Father's love.

THROUGH ALL LIFE'S CHANGING SEASONS

In the springtime of our youth, we take for granted
the sunny, happy moments of our days.
Then summer comes, with its love and warmth and laughter,
and life seems one extended song of praise.

But those rainbow seasons cannot last forever,
and one day we realize we're growing old;
The springtime of our years has finally faded,
and the summer sun has turned to autumn's gold.

We seem to feel life slipping through our fingers,
and we clutch each moment tightly till it's gone,
Wishing we could somehow stop time's passing
and make this present joy shine on and on.

Let's be thankful that our lives were planned and fashioned
by a God of no beginning and no end,
A God to whom a lifetime is a brief touch,
no more than one soft whisper on the wind.

For this God, Lord of all life's changing seasons,
Lord of everything that's been and what will be,
Has promised us, when winter's finally over,
an endless spring in His eternity.

He has made everything beautiful
in its time.

ECCLESIASTES 3:11

LORD OF THE CHANGING SEASONS OF MY LIFE . . .

There is a beauty, a quiet splendor,
in the journey of maturity when we travel with You . . .
year by year, season by season, growing closer,
becoming more and more Your servant and Your friend.
Help me, Lord, to live so closely to Your truth,
so completely in Your will,
that wisdom lines my spirit as time lines my face.
Keep my heart forever young, my hope in You unfailing.
Let me age in autumn colors,
dressed in banners of Your love.

WEDDING DAY

Here she comes, Lord, on her father's arm,
walking down the aisle,
The future in her shining eyes,
a tremble in her smile . . .
And I suddenly recall the day she gave her heart to You.

There she stands, Lord, at her bridegroom's side,
the two of them together
Looking young and brave and hopeful
as they vow to love forever . . .
And I tearfully recall the day she gave her heart to You.

Now she turns, Lord, and as I behold
the radiance in her face,
I somehow know it was Your plan
that brought her to this place . . .
And I thankfully recall the day she gave her heart to You

There she goes, Lord, down the aisle again,
a woman and a wife,
And I sense Your benediction
as I thank You for her life . . .
And I joyfully recall the day she gave her heart to You.

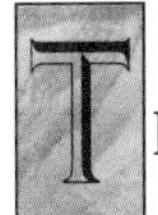

The promise is for you and your children. . . .

ACTS 2:39

BELOVED FATHER . . .

Thank You for the blessing of my family,
the assurance that they belong to You,
that they are dear to You,
that they are safe with You.
Keep them,
that my children's children
may know Your steadfast love.

SHE REMEMBERS . . .

he remembers . . .

When her hands didn't tremble and her eyes were still bright
With a young girl's first dreams and young love's first light,
When she walked down the aisle as a hopeful new bride
With the future before her and the world open wide . . .

When her steps were still sure and her back was still strong,
When her arms held a baby and her heart held a song,
When she thrived in her role as a mother and wife
And the needs of her family gave purpose to life . . .

When home was a haven where everyone came,
And loved ones still hugged her and called her by name,
When her opinion still mattered, her advice was still sought,
When she was a person, and not just a thought . . .

When each day was a gift, a treasure to hold,
Not just long hours of loneliness spent growing old. . . .
In her bed by the window, with nothing to see,
She remembers a lifetime of loving. . . .
Do we?

The memory of the righteous
will be a blessing.

PROVERBS 10:7

LORD OF YESTERDAY, TODAY, AND TOMORROW . . .

Help me to remember
those who might be easy to forget—
those who go unnoticed . . . and unloved.
Let me take the time to see, to smile, to touch,
to hug, to hold a hand,
or just sit quietly and be there,
to ease the loneliness
and be a comforting reminder that
You care.

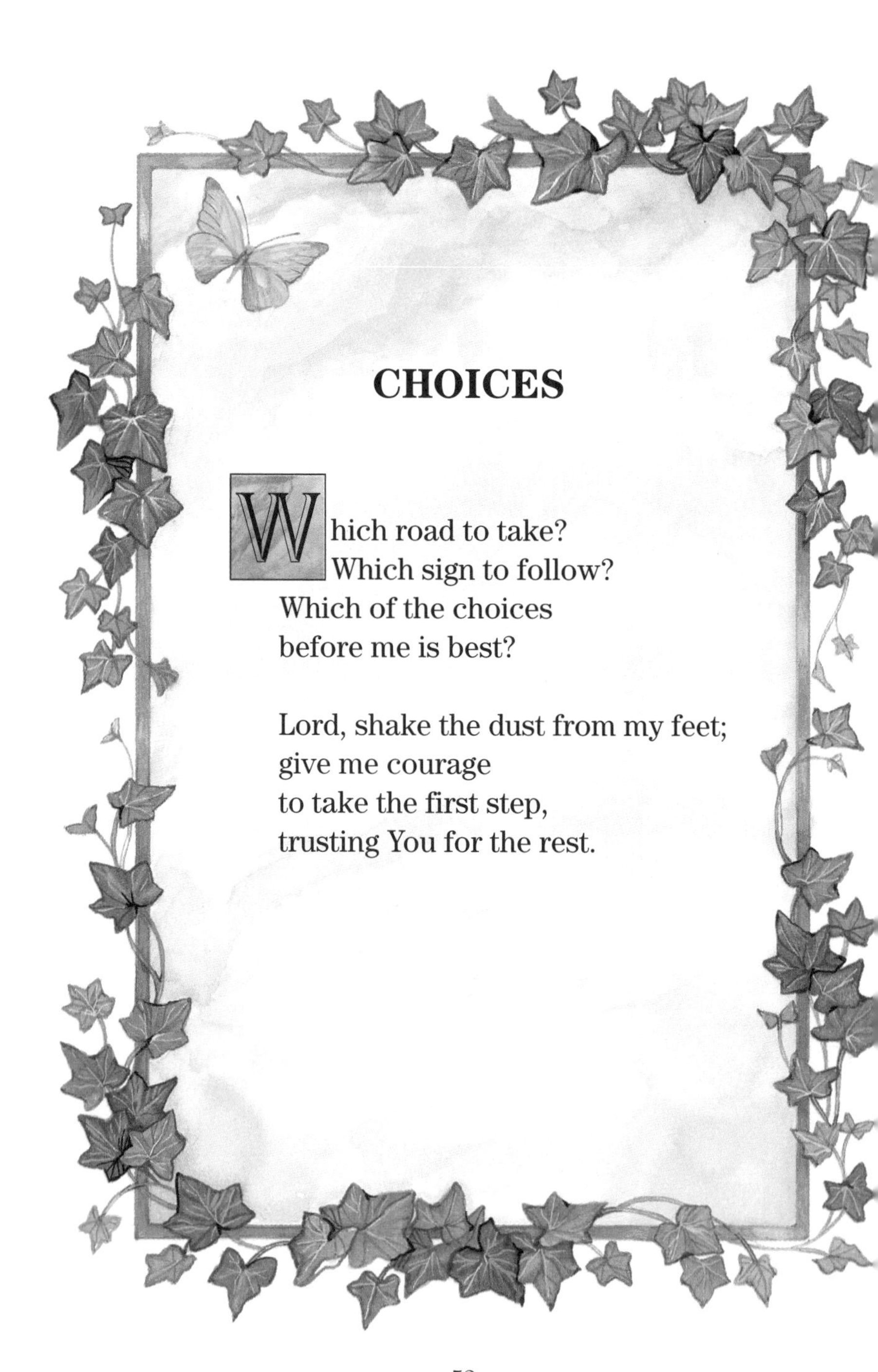

CHOICES

Which road to take?
Which sign to follow?
Which of the choices
before me is best?

Lord, shake the dust from my feet;
give me courage
to take the first step,
trusting You for the rest.

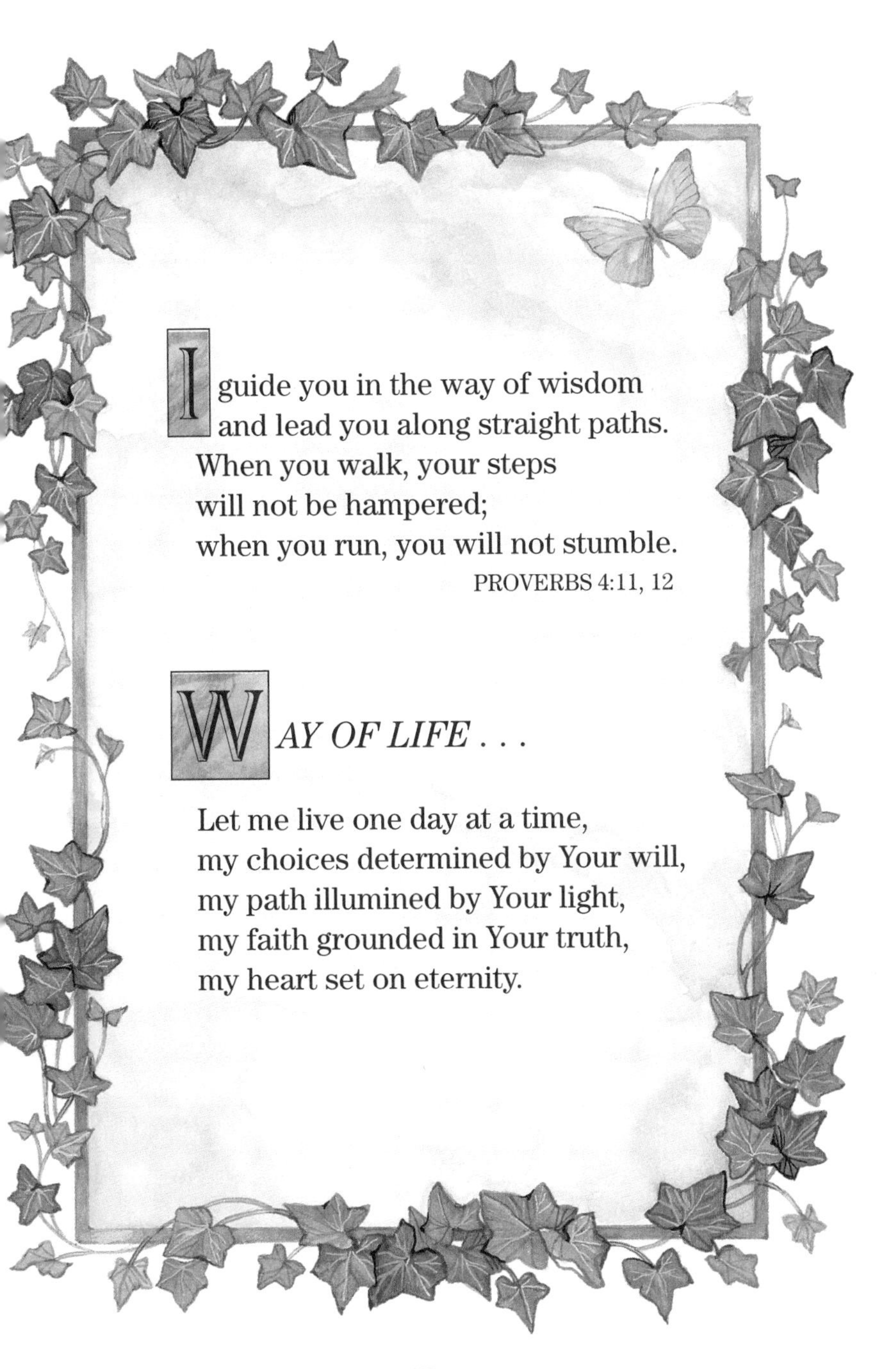

I guide you in the way of wisdom
and lead you along straight paths.
When you walk, your steps
will not be hampered;
when you run, you will not stumble.

PROVERBS 4:11, 12

WAY OF LIFE . . .

Let me live one day at a time,
my choices determined by Your will,
my path illumined by Your light,
my faith grounded in Your truth,
my heart set on eternity.

WHEN OUR HEROES HAVE ALL GONE

When we're parted from our family,
Separated from our friends,
When it seems as though the world has turned away,
We're so quick to get discouraged,
Even frightened for ourselves,
And it's difficult to see beyond today.

When everyone we used to count on,
Everything we thought secure,
Is removed, and we're left, reeling on our own,
What do we do then?
How do we keep from giving up?
Are we really meant to live life all alone?

In the midst of our confusion
And despair, there comes a voice,
Whispering softly at the entrance to the heart,
"Child, your heroes have all gone,
But I'm still here. Remember Me?
I've been with you all along, right from the start.

"Life will bring you many partings
Through the years, but be assured
You will never have to say good-bye to Me.
Put Me first, above all others,
For I'm the only friend you have
Who will be with you throughout eternity."

he Lord is near to all who call on him. . . .

PSALM 145:18

Come near to God and he will come near to you.

JAMES 4:8

Remain in me, and I will remain in you.

JOHN 15:4

*Y CONSTANT COMPANION . . .*

You are faithful and unfailing,
 a Forever Friend.
Forgive me for all the times
I've looked elsewhere for security,
 founding my hope on people or things,
when in my heart I know there is no real refuge but You.

LIFE GIFTS

Thank You for my yesterdays,
the memories that I cherish,
those precious moments captured
by the heart throughout the years.
Thank You for Your guidance through
the trials and the triumphs—
Your presence was unfailing
through the good times and the tears.

Thank You for the promise
that You hold all my tomorrows
securely in Your hand
as You walk with me on the way.
Most of all, Lord, thank You
for this present hour of blessing,
for the splendor of this shining gift—
the glory of today.

This is the day the Lord has made;
let us rejoice and be glad in it.

PSALM 118:24

Jesus Christ is the same yesterday
and today and forever.

HEBREWS 13:8

LORD OF MY LIFE . . .

Where would I be today, Lord,
if You had not been
in my yesterdays?
How could I face the future
without You?

Thank You for filling my past
and my present with Your love
and Your grace
and Your mercy. . . .

Thank You for Your promise
that I will spend
all my tomorrows
with You.

DECEMBER SONG

What song will I sing
when the winter of my years
has come upon me?
A lament for mistakes made,
kindnesses left undone,
harsh words inflicted,
loved ones neglected?
Or an anthem of praise
for every springtime beauty given,
every rose of summer savored,
every autumn harvest blessed
and gathered in?

Lord, in the winter of my years,
may the song be sweet
and swollen with gladness—
a song of celebration,
a psalm of joy,
for a life lived in harmony
with the Creator and His created,
a life in which love gave the rhythm
to every day of every season . . .
a life whose winter is an *Alleluia*,
a triumphant overture to eternal spring.

here is a time for everything,
and a season for every activity under heaven.

ECCLESIASTES 3:1

I know that there is nothing better
for men than to be happy and do good
while they live.

ECCLESIASTES 3:12

ORD GOD . . .

You who are the Alpha and the Omega,
the Beginning and the End . . .

Make of my days a song to delight Your heart.
Make my life a *Gloria*,
a celebration of Your love.

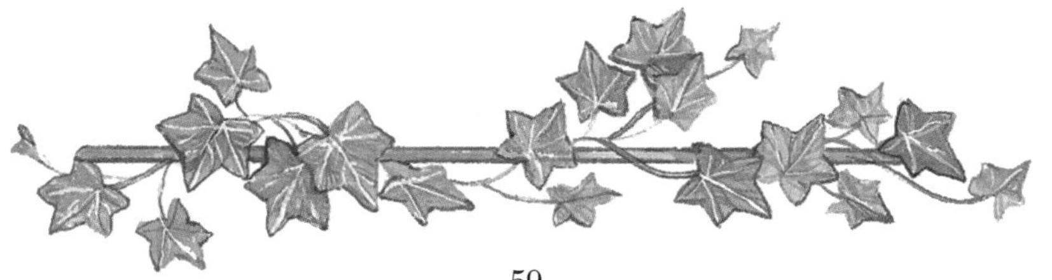

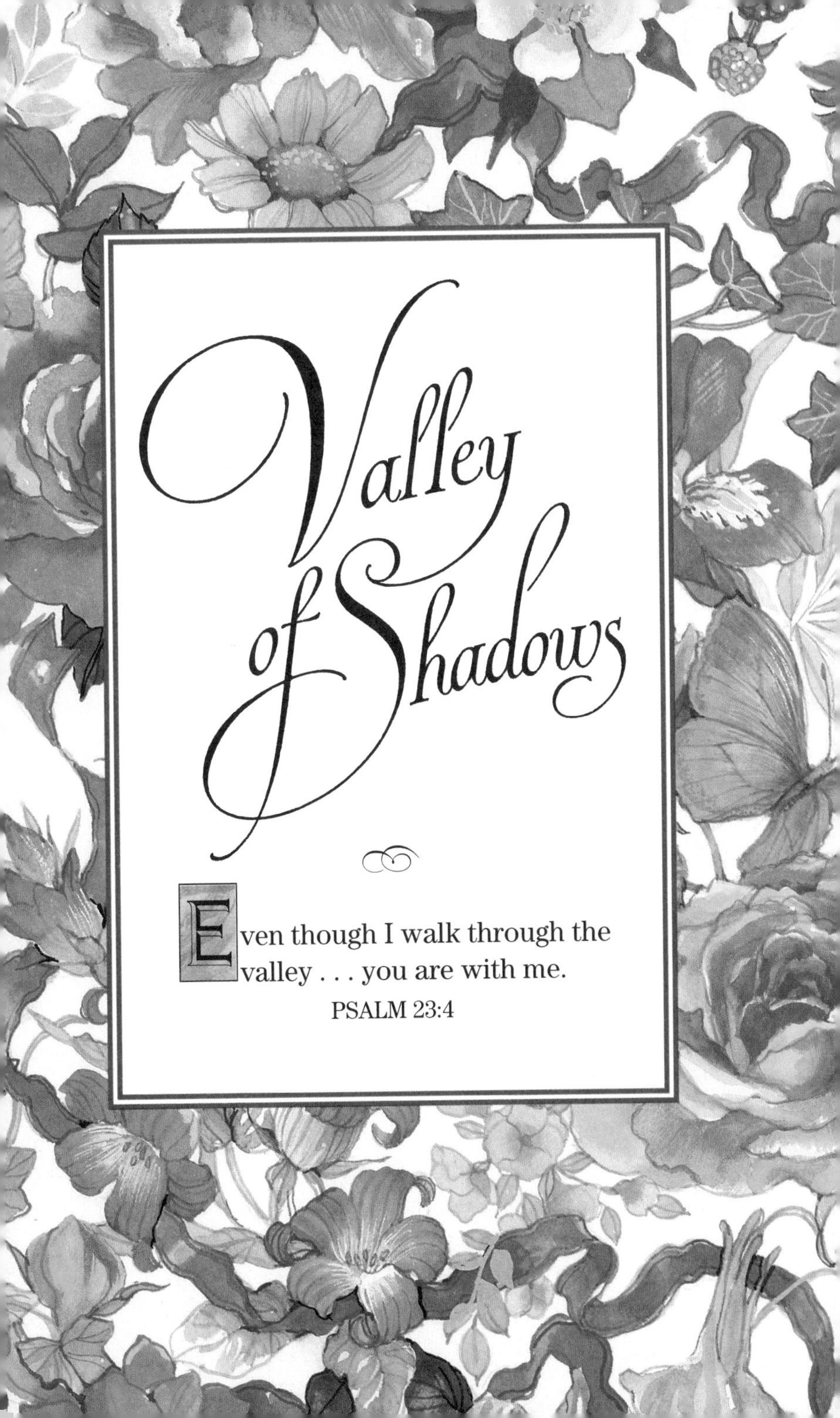

Valley of Shadows

Even though I walk through the valley . . . you are with me.

PSALM 23:4

ELIJAH . . .

THE HIDING PLACE

The Lord said, "Go out and stand on the mountain in the presence of the Lord, for the Lord is about to pass by."

Then a great and powerful wind tore the mountains apart and shattered the rocks before the Lord, but the Lord was not in the wind. After the wind there was an earthquake, but the Lord was not in the earthquake. After the earthquake came a fire, but the Lord was not in the fire. And after the fire came a gentle whisper.

1 KINGS 19:11-13

Elijah . . . Confronter of evil,
Defender of Truth,
Champion of the Lord,
A prophet who towered above other prophets.
Ravens fed him,
angels served him,
and God approved him.

A man of miracles,
he turned a handful of meal
and a little oil into an abundant supply,
restored a widow's son from death to life,
and called down fire from heaven
to consume Baal's altars and declare Jehovah King.

Yet in the face of fear,
Elijah fled to the wilderness,
sank down under a broom tree
and prayed to die.
Lonely and discouraged,
he remembered the trials
and forgot the triumphs,
giving in at last to self-pity and despair.

But then God came . . .
not in the windstorm,
not in the earthquake,
not in the fire,
but in a gentle whisper
as soft as silence.

In a still, small voice,
God spoke to Elijah,
reminding him that he wasn't alone.
The Lord and the faithful
were still his companions.

In the silence, God whispered
words of comfort and guidance
and gave a new call.
Then a still small voice
sent Elijah forth . . .
Confronter of evil,
Defender of Truth,
Champion of the Lord.

THE PROMISE

Who has not known . . .
the defeat of expectations,
the delay of answered prayer,
the dark times when the heart gives in
to doubting and despair . . .
Times when disappointment nags us
and discouragement sets in,
when our thoughts are dominated
by the things that might have been.

We expect life to be fair,
and when it's not, we blame the One
who gave us everlasting life
by giving us His Son.
Somehow we've missed the truth
that God and life are not the same—
when life is hard, we seem to think
the Lord should get the blame.

We accuse our Suffering Saviour
of the wrongs this world inflicts;
we indict the Man of Sorrows
for Satan's evil tricks.
Yet belonging to the God of Love
is not a guarantee
of life without affliction
or a world that's trouble-free.

Our peace would be a feeble thing
if we could bear no pain;
if our hope were based on happiness,
our faith would be in vain.
Lord, help us understand that,
though Your promises are true,
You never pledged an easy life
to those who walk with You.

Help us to remember
we must always count the cost,
that being Your disciples
will eventually mean a cross.
The only promise we can cling to
when the storms of life assail
is that You'll go through them with us—
and Your love will still prevail.

When you pass through the rivers,
they will not sweep over you.
When you walk through the fire, you will not be burned.

ISAIAH 43:2

OMFORTING SAVIOUR . . .

Forgive me for those times I have blamed You
for my problems or turned away from You in my despair.
Even then, Your love sustained me, refused to let me go.
Though I know the world will fail me, Lord,
I know You never will.
You have promised to be with me in all things.

FOR THE LONELY

When the only sound in the room
is the echo of a lonely heart
crying out in protest against the silence—
God cares.

When the only thing to look forward to
is the nighttime, because for a few fleeting hours
you can forget—
God cares.

When the only dream you can cling to
is the one that takes you back to yesterday,
before the pain—
God cares.

When the voice you long to hear
and the smile you yearn to see
can only be found among your memories—
God cares.

In your cry for comfort,
in your need for communion,
in your search for peace and a glimpse of hope—
with a Father's heart, a Father's love,
God cares.

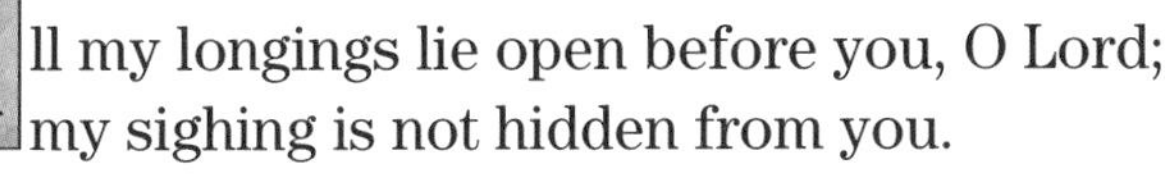

All my longings lie open before you, O Lord;
my sighing is not hidden from you.

PSALM 38:9

I, even I, am he who comforts you.

ISAIAH 51:12

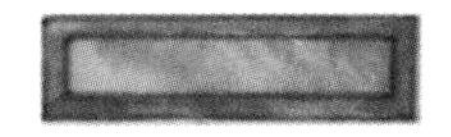

FAITHFUL COMFORTER AND FRIEND . . .

I thank You for the assurance
of Your presence,
the solace to be found
by just . . . abiding.
When I forget Your promise, Lord,
remind me that I'm never alone,
that in all things life brings,
You are there.

LIKE A RIVER

Like a great and mighty river is the Spirit,
flowing through God's people who believe.
His power is ours in fullness beyond measure,
continually pouring out as we receive.

Though obstacles may rise and block its passage,
slow it down, or modify its course,
There's nothing that can halt its steady flowing,
for the Living Water is the river's source.

Life's struggles won't impede God's stream of mercy
if we trust God's love to always make a way,
And the river will flow out from us to others,
if we keep our eyes on Jesus day by day.

I will make rivers flow on barren heights,
and springs within the valleys.
I will turn the desert into pools of water,
and the parched ground into springs.

ISAIAH 41:18

Whoever believes in me, as the Scripture has said,
streams of living water will flow from within him.

JOHN 7:38

MY LOVING LORD . . .

When my faith would fail or falter
under the difficulties of life,
let me keep my eyes on You,
the blessed Source of all life.

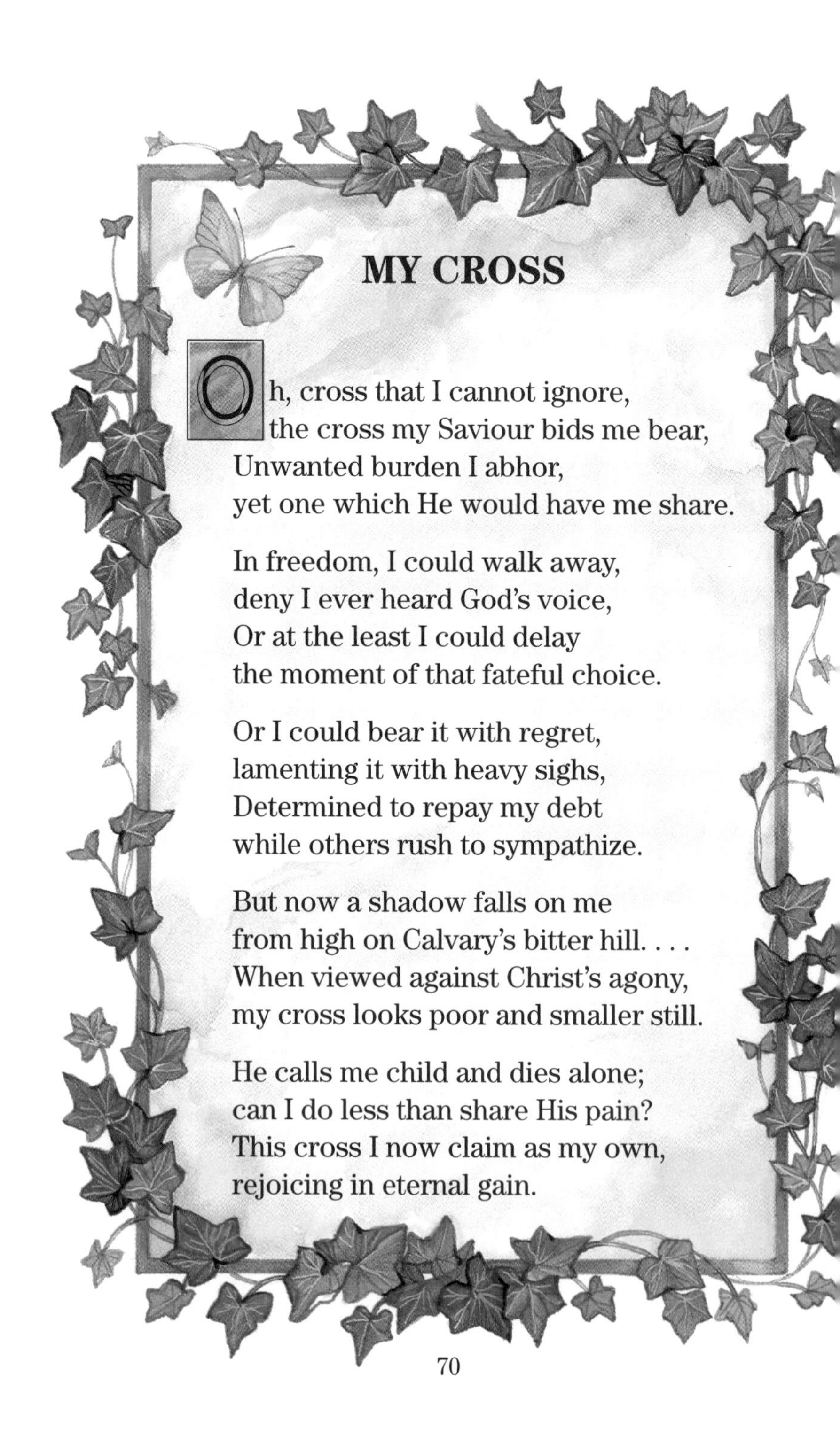

MY CROSS

Oh, cross that I cannot ignore,
the cross my Saviour bids me bear,
Unwanted burden I abhor,
yet one which He would have me share.

In freedom, I could walk away,
deny I ever heard God's voice,
Or at the least I could delay
the moment of that fateful choice.

Or I could bear it with regret,
lamenting it with heavy sighs,
Determined to repay my debt
while others rush to sympathize.

But now a shadow falls on me
from high on Calvary's bitter hill. . . .
When viewed against Christ's agony,
my cross looks poor and smaller still.

He calls me child and dies alone;
can I do less than share His pain?
This cross I now claim as my own,
rejoicing in eternal gain.

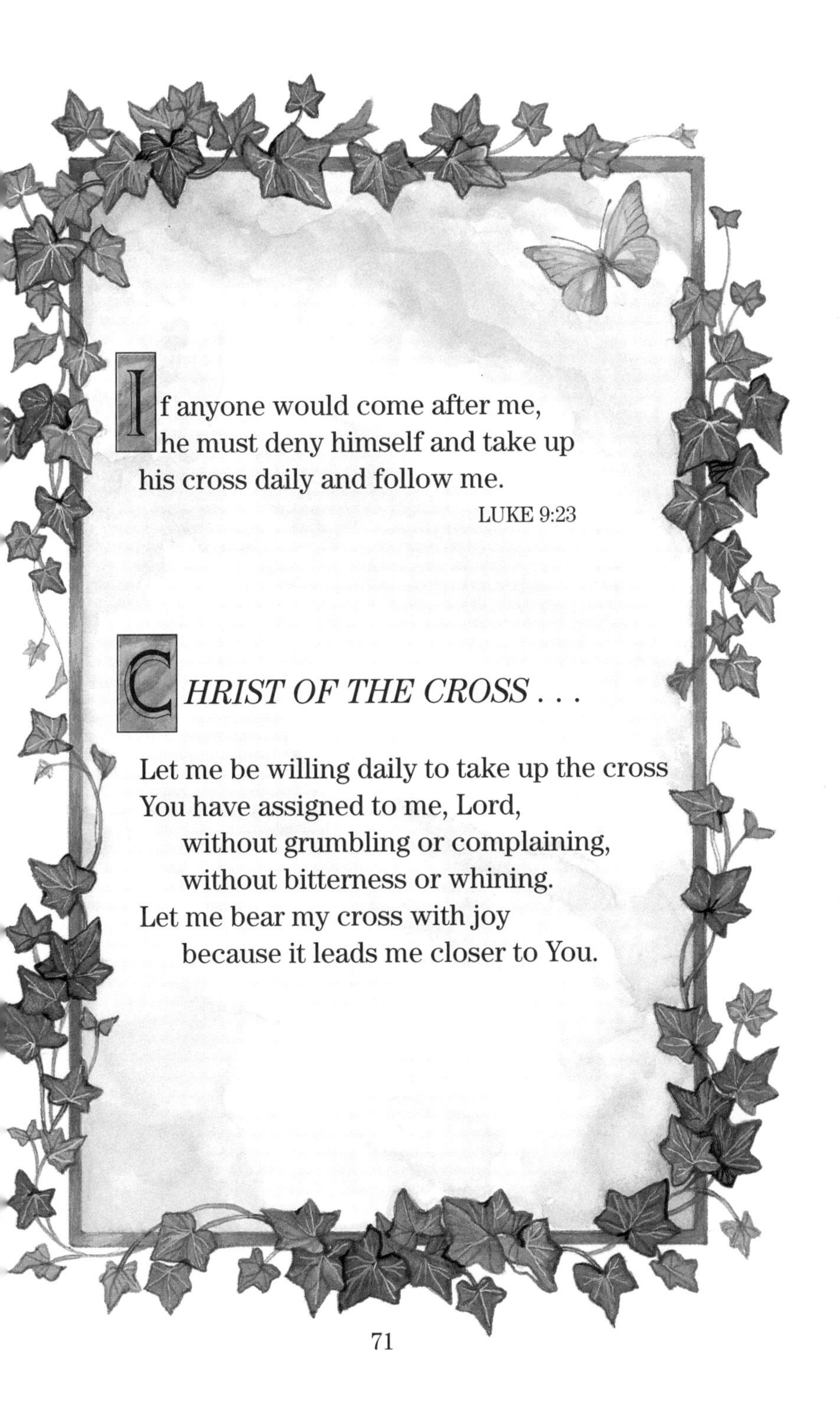

If anyone would come after me,
he must deny himself and take up
his cross daily and follow me.

LUKE 9:23

CHRIST OF THE CROSS . . .

Let me be willing daily to take up the cross
You have assigned to me, Lord,
without grumbling or complaining,
without bitterness or whining.
Let me bear my cross with joy
because it leads me closer to You.

A FRIEND FOR ALL

For the one who feels rejected,
For the child who's been neglected,
For the desperate wife, tormented and abused . . .
For the prodigal in exile,
Victim of a sinful lifestyle,
For the aged, often frightened and confused . . .
For the lonely and the homeless,
For the helpless and the hopeless,
For the suffering whose affliction knows no end . . .
There is One who waits to hold you,
Reassure you and console you;
Jesus loves you as a Father and a Friend.

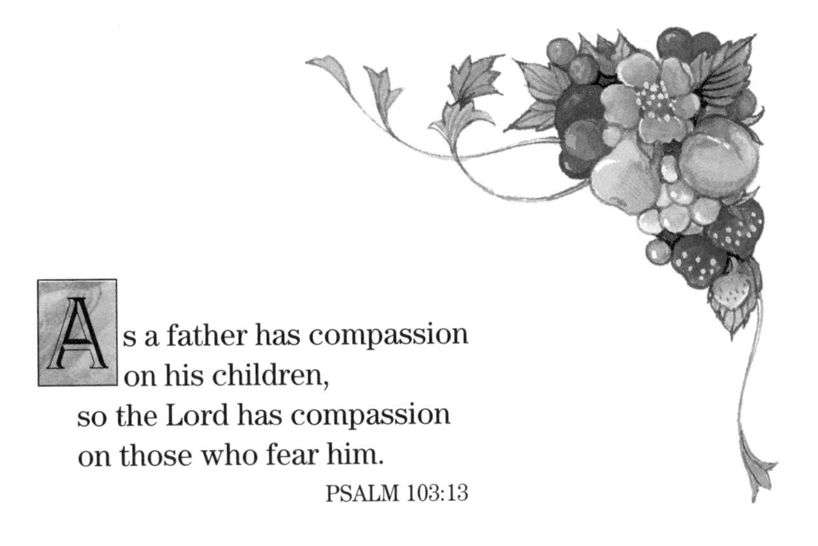

As a father has compassion
on his children,
so the Lord has compassion
on those who fear him.

PSALM 103:13

MERCIFUL FATHER,
COMPASSIONATE FRIEND . . .

Thank You for Your love—
a love available to all,
a love without condition or demands.
Thank You for the assurance
that You care about our needs,
that You hear our cry for help,
and will comfort and deliver
those who call.

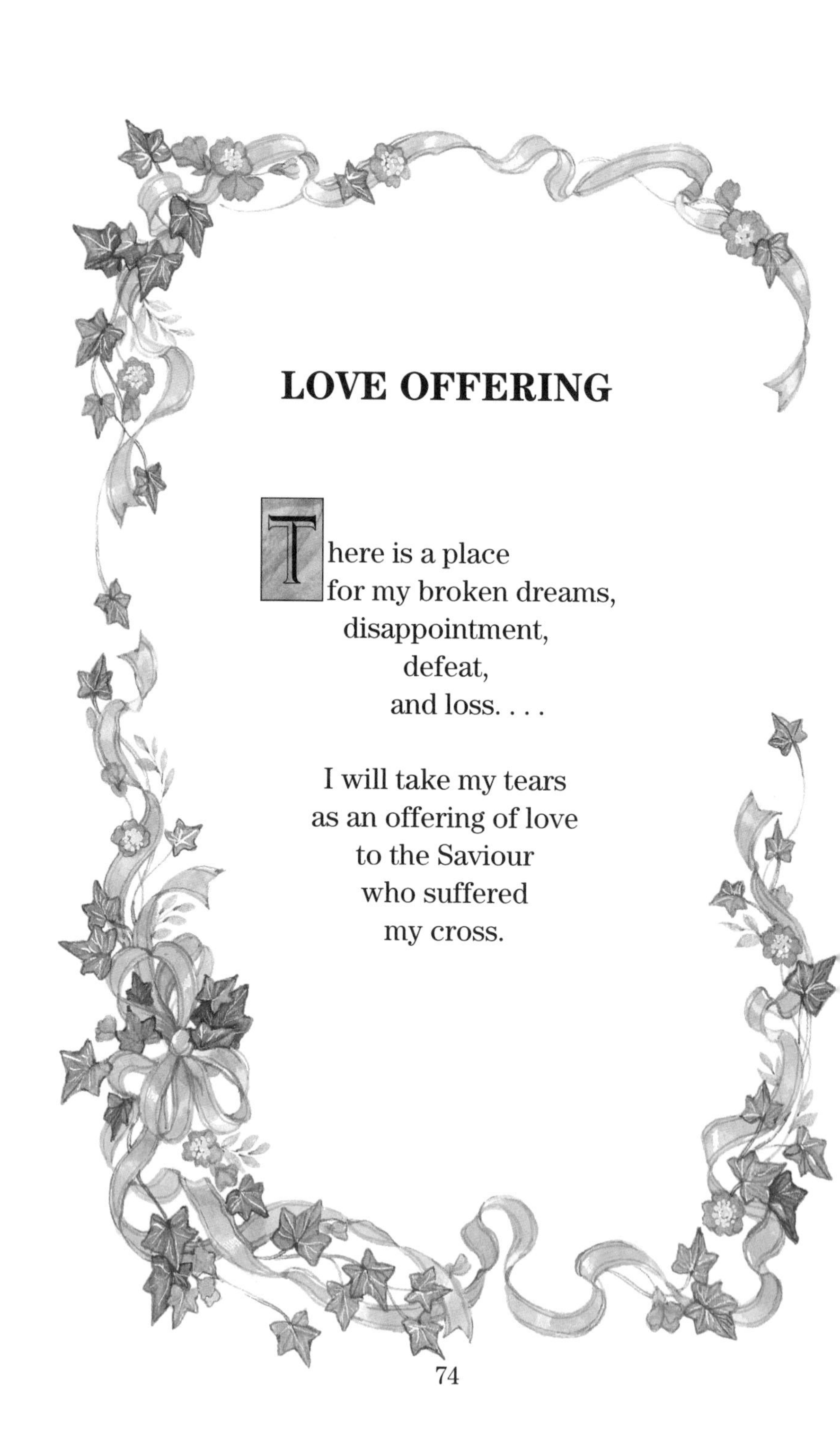

LOVE OFFERING

There is a place
for my broken dreams,
disappointment,
defeat,
and loss. . . .

I will take my tears
as an offering of love
to the Saviour
who suffered
my cross.

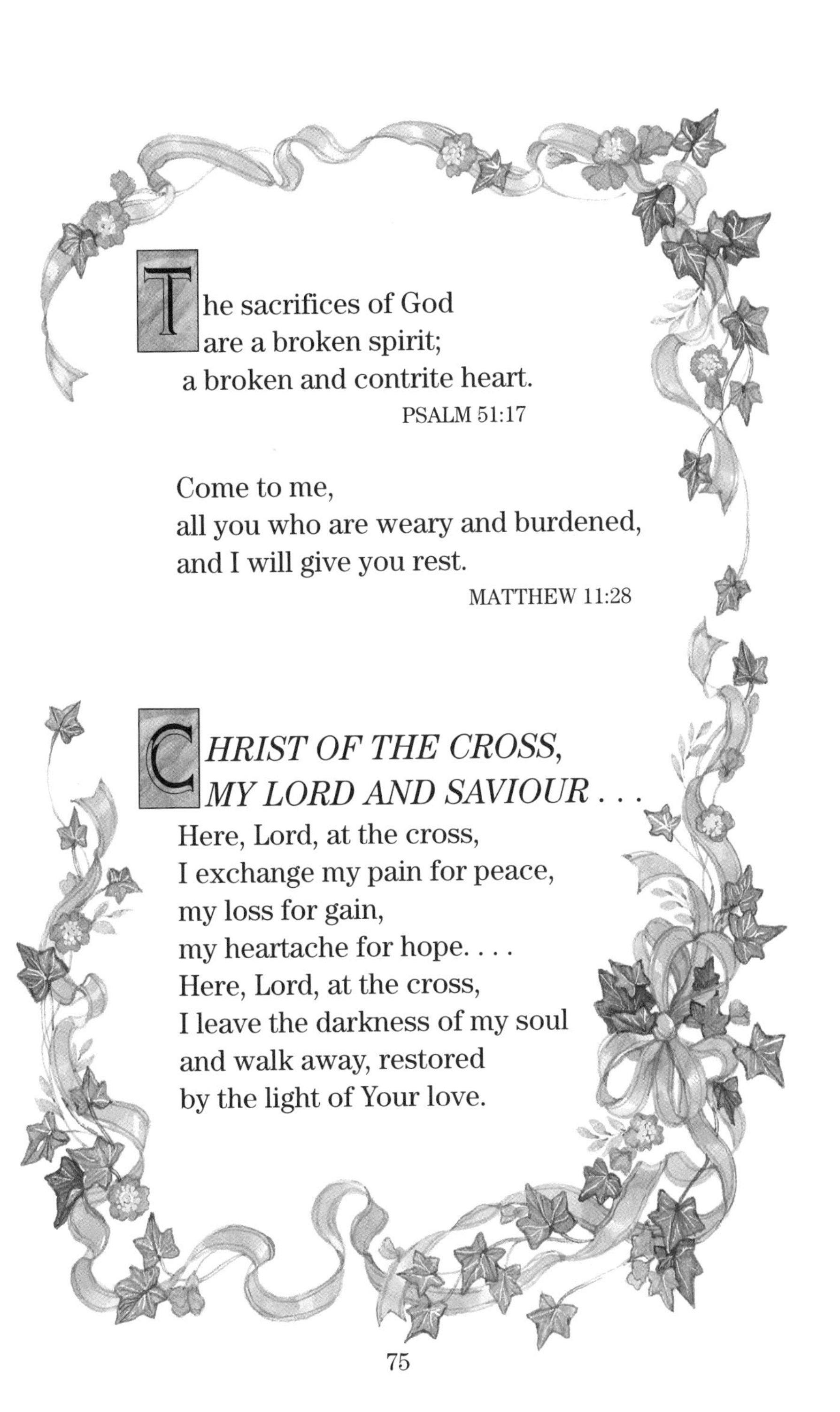

The sacrifices of God
are a broken spirit;
a broken and contrite heart.

PSALM 51:17

Come to me,
all you who are weary and burdened,
and I will give you rest.

MATTHEW 11:28

*CHRIST OF THE CROSS,
MY LORD AND SAVIOUR . . .*

Here, Lord, at the cross,
I exchange my pain for peace,
my loss for gain,
my heartache for hope. . . .
Here, Lord, at the cross,
I leave the darkness of my soul
and walk away, restored
by the light of Your love.

OUTSIDE THE CIRCLE

Some dress their loneliness in bright, carefree hues,
wrappings that deny the wrenching anguish of the heart
Painted smiles.
Busy schedules.
Power jobs.
Lavish houses filled with proofs of their success.

Others, like the world's abandoned children,
stand outside with wounded eyes, looking in.
Spurned.
Rejected.
In despair.
Barren lives, where no one notices or cares.

For those outside the circle, there is One who understands,
Who knows just what it means to walk alone.
He was scorned.
Forsaken.
Deserted, even in death.

To Him, you're *Someone* . . . someone special . . .
A child to cherish.
A friend to nurture and to love.
You belong.

To Him, your life has meaning. . . .
For love of you, the Saviour hung upon a cross.
You are unique.
Beloved.
Never alone.

"I am with you," Jesus promised.
"Always with you . . . to the end."

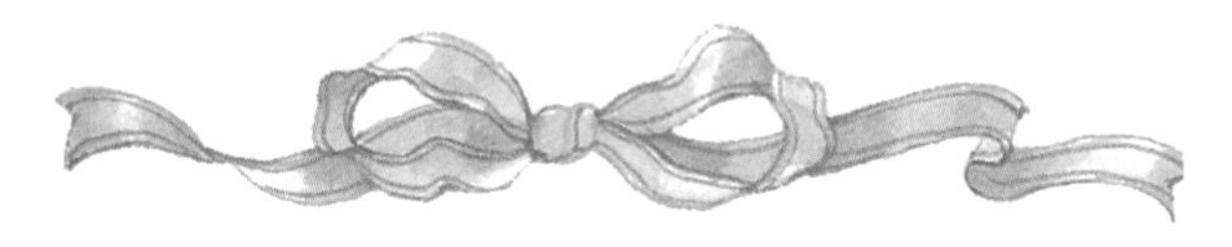

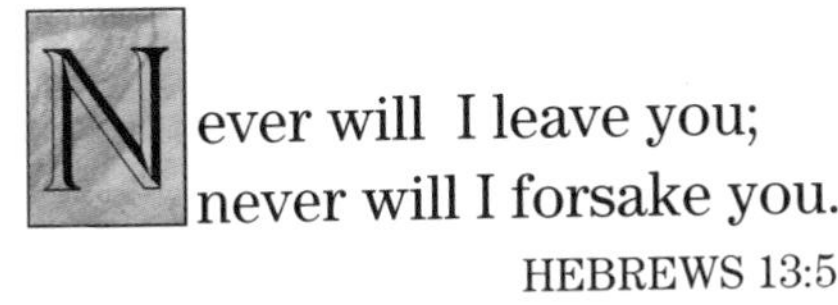

Never will I leave you;
never will I forsake you.
HEBREWS 13:5

I will be with you always,
to the very end of the age.
MATTHEW 28:20

LORD OF ALL COMFORT, FAITHFUL FRIEND . . .

When loneliness would enshroud my heart,
Your love casts aside the gloom
and replaces it with warmth and light
and compassion.
When I'm feeling forsaken, abandoned, alone,
You gently touch me to remind me
that You're with me . . . always with me . . .
to the end.

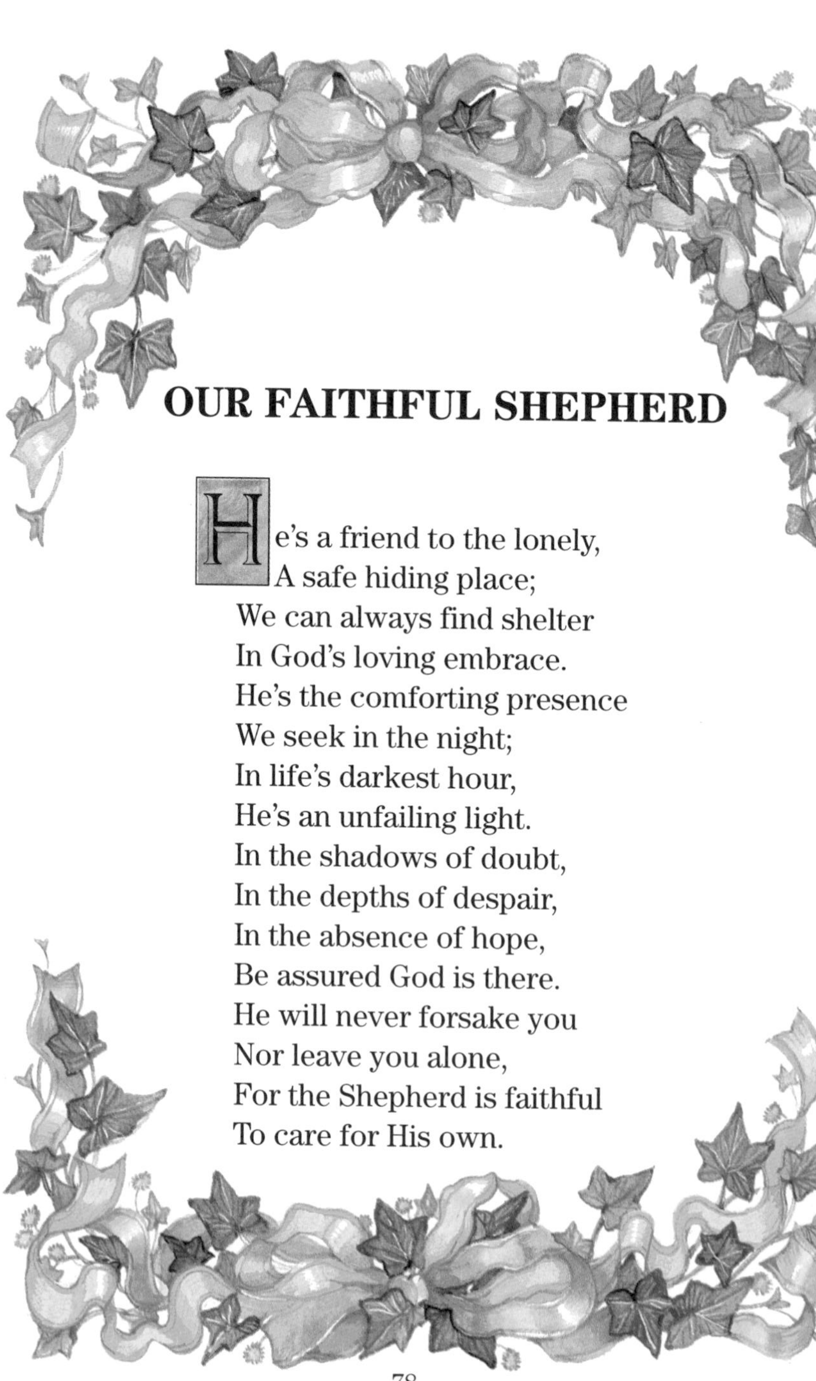

OUR FAITHFUL SHEPHERD

He's a friend to the lonely,
A safe hiding place;
We can always find shelter
In God's loving embrace.
He's the comforting presence
We seek in the night;
In life's darkest hour,
He's an unfailing light.
In the shadows of doubt,
In the depths of despair,
In the absence of hope,
Be assured God is there.
He will never forsake you
Nor leave you alone,
For the Shepherd is faithful
To care for His own.

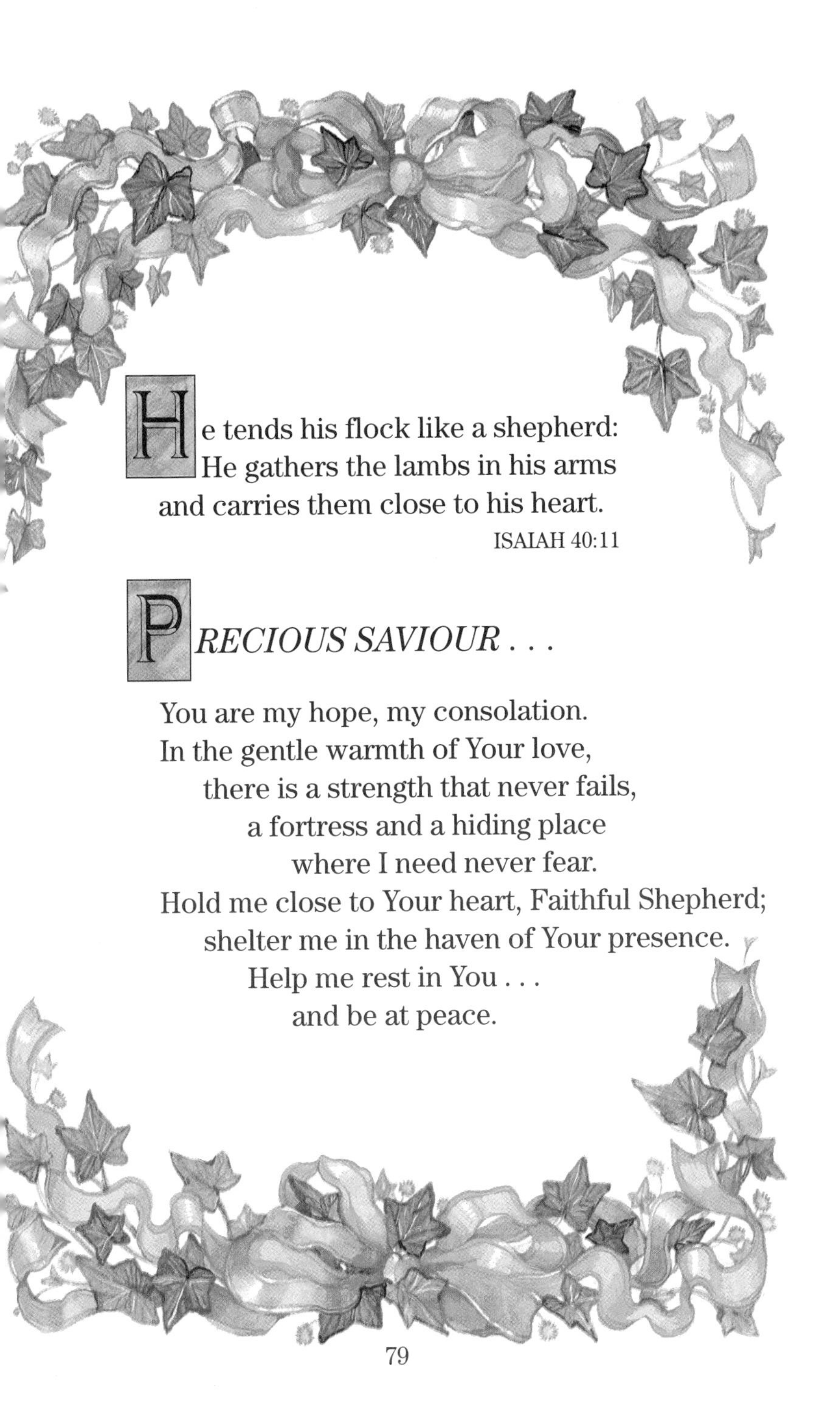

He tends his flock like a shepherd:
He gathers the lambs in his arms
and carries them close to his heart.

ISAIAH 40:11

PRECIOUS SAVIOUR . . .

You are my hope, my consolation.
In the gentle warmth of Your love,
there is a strength that never fails,
a fortress and a hiding place
where I need never fear.
Hold me close to Your heart, Faithful Shepherd;
shelter me in the haven of Your presence.
Help me rest in You . . .
and be at peace.

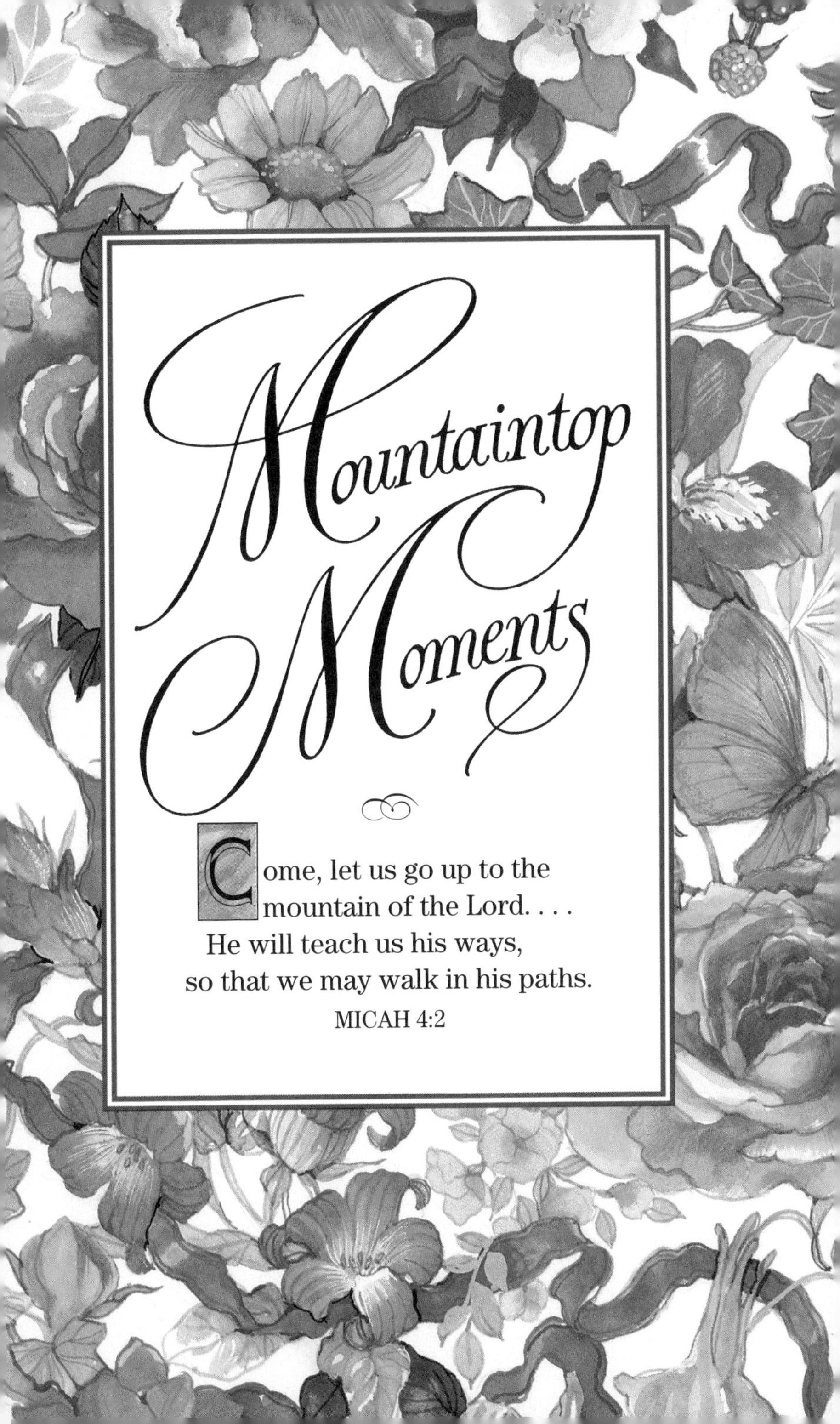

Mountaintop Moments

Come, let us go up to the
mountain of the Lord. . . .
He will teach us his ways,
so that we may walk in his paths.

MICAH 4:2

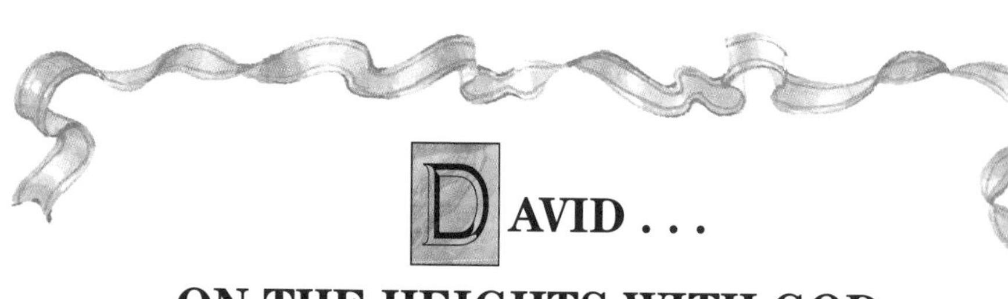

DAVID . . .

ON THE HEIGHTS WITH GOD

He makes my feet like the feet of a deer;
he enables me to stand on the heights.

PSALM 18:33

He set my feet on a rock and gave me a firm place to stand. He put a new song in my mouth, a hymn of praise to our God.

PSALM 40:2, 3

David . . . A simple shepherd boy, anointed,
appointed by God to be king . . .
slayer of giants, leader of nations,
ruler of the people of the Lord.

This warrior-king, fierce against the foe,
found his heart's own contentment
in gentle things like music
and poetry and praise.

A man of noble character: wise leader, loyal patriot,
royal statesman, devoted friend.
He fought for God's honor with relentless resolve,
yet showed mercy to a treacherous enemy
and an unfaithful son.
He was a generous ruler with integrity of heart,
a man of humility and deep sensitivity.

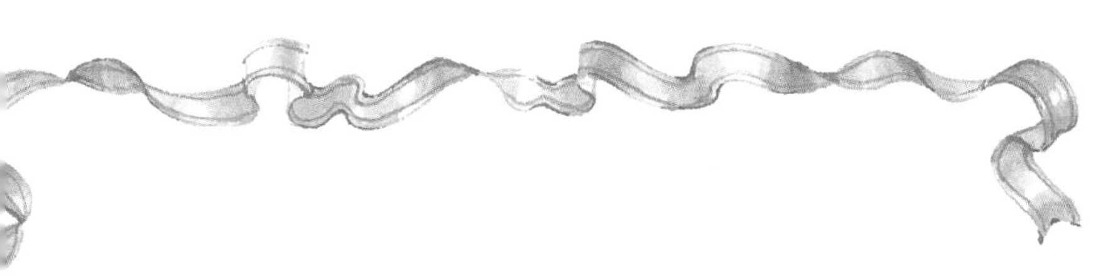

Valiant in spirit,
he survived the hardships of the wilderness,
endured the agonies of exile,
braved the terrors of war.

Weak in the flesh,
he succumbed to the corruption of power
and the deception of sin.
His passions carved out in his heart
an unsanctified place where the darkness set in
and reigned.

Yet through it all—
the successes and defeats, the triumphs and failures,
among the monuments and amid the ruins—
he sought for God.

His sins were many, his weaknesses grave.
At the end, his family betrayed him,
his followers deserted him,
his kingdom crumbled,
his dignity fled.
But even then, God called him His own
and bound his wounds.

In the valley of the shadows, or beside still waters,
in the pit of despair, or on the heights of joy,
David clung to God with one steadfast hope
and sang his songs of praise.

MOUNTAINTOP

This is my place of celebration,
my mountaintop—
Not in the mystic or the fantastic,
not in a work of wonder or upon a pinnacle of power,
not even in a poured-out sacrifice of praise—
But here, in this ordinary place, where all is quiet
before the clamor of the day
rushes headlong toward me. . . .
Here, where the only music is the sighing of the wind,
where the only mystery is the heartbeat of my life,
where the only wonders are the commonplace things
touched by the glory of Your love.
Here I stand, rejoicing in Your presence,
in awe of Your goodness, amazed by Your grace,
in this place of daily celebration with You.

You will fill me with joy
in your presence.

PSALM 16:11

Rejoice in the Lord always.

PHILIPPIANS 4:4

CHRIST, THE SOURCE OF MY JOY . . .

Let me not wait for the right place,
the right time,
to celebrate Your presence.
Let me go rejoicing through my days,
abiding in You and delighting in You,
praising You now and forever.

HIGH PLACES

God calls me away from the clamor and crowds,
Bids me to come to His side,
Implores me to cease from my worthless endeavors,
To flee to His arms, and abide.

God lifts me above the world's noise and confusion,
Setting me firmly in place
On the heights in His presence, where I can rejoice
In God's marvelous goodness and grace.

e enables me to go on the heights.

HABAKKUK 3:19

BLESSED LORD,
MY FIRM FOUNDATION . . .

Any place with You, Lord,
is a blessed place. . . .
Any time in Your presence
is a season of rejoicing.
Thank You for bringing a touch of Your glory,
a gift of Your love, to the small things
and the everyday places of my life.

GOD AMONG US

THE BELOVED SON
became a baby;
THE ANOINTED ONE
came down to save.
THE GREAT HIGH PRIEST
was made a shepherd;
THE PRINCE OF PEACE
defied the grave.
THE RIGHTEOUS JUDGE
became a ransom;
THE LION OF JUDAH
bore our shame.
THE KING OF KINGS
was crowned with briars;
JESUS, SAVIOUR,
we praise Your name.

The Word became flesh
and lived for a while among us.

JOHN 1:14

IMMANUEL . . .
GOD WITH US . . .

At Your name, Lord—
Your precious name—
my heart bows,
my soul exults,
my spirit rejoices.
May all that I am,
all that You created me to be,
celebrate the wondrous name
of JESUS.

ABIDING JOY

There are times, Lord, when You lead me
to the mountain to rejoice,
Times You give my heart a song,
my happiness a voice.
There are times within the valley
when it's difficult to praise,
But then You point me to the splendor
of my ordinary days.
There are times when shadows fall
and darkness seems to hide Your light,
But then Your love comes gently,
like a star upon the night.
There are times of exultation,
simple, quiet moments, too—
And I live in celebration of them all . . .
Because of You.

Be joyful always; pray continually;
give thanks in all circumstances,
for this is God's will for you in Christ Jesus.

1 THESSALONIANS 5:16-18

Praise the Lord, O my soul;
all my inmost being, praise his holy name.
Praise the Lord, O my soul,
and forget not all his benefits.

PSALM 103:1, 2

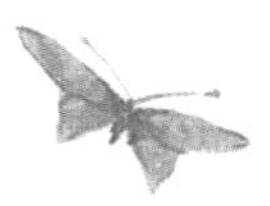

LORD OF ALL TIMES AND ALL SEASONS . . .

Thank You for those mountaintop moments
when my spirit soars and my heart sings.
But thank You even more, Lord,
for the quiet days, the simple, ordinary days,
even for the difficult, shadowed days,
when time and time again
You prove that Your faithfulness is unfailing
and Your love is for always.

CELEBRATION OF GOD'S LOVE

God's love is the one
lasting gift of perfection—
A wonder, a glory,
the truest reflection
Of His caring heart
for the world He created—
God's love is a gift
Meant to be celebrated.

his is how we know what love is:
Jesus Christ laid down his life for us.

1 JOHN 3:16

This is love: not that we loved God,
but that he loved us and sent his Son
as an atoning sacrifice for our sins.

1 JOHN 4:10

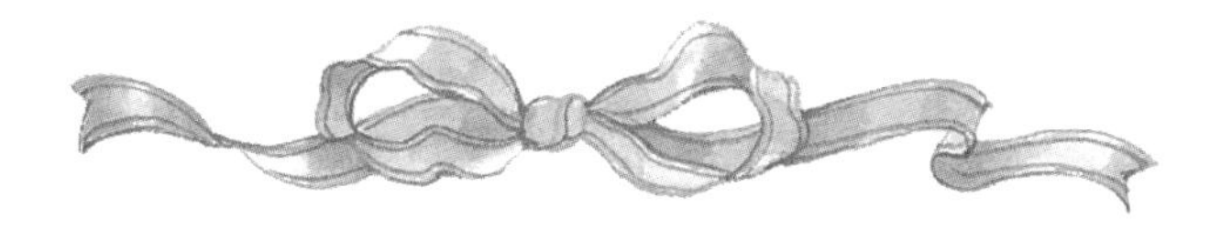

*OVING FATHER . . .*

Make my life, day by day,
a song of thanksgiving,
an offering of praise,
a celebration of Your love.

ANTHEM

Give my heart a voice
to tell the world about my Saviour—
Give my soul a song
that will ring across the years,
A song that sings Your boundless love
in sunshine or in shadow,
A psalm of praise for all my days,
through happiness or tears.

Make my life a melody
in tune with all creation—
Help me live in harmony
with every living thing.
Let my whole existence
be an anthem of rejoicing,
A prelude to eternal life
with You, my Lord and King.

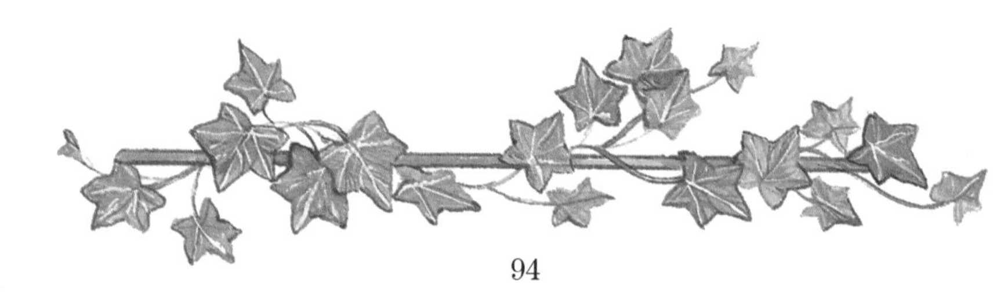

My heart is stirred
by a noble theme
as I recite my verses for the king. . . .
I will perpetuate your memory
through all generations.

PSALM 45:1, 17

BLESSED SAVIOUR,
KING ETERNAL . . .

The only way I know
to thank You, Lord,
for what You've done for me
is to carry Your praise
on my lips
from now to eternity. . . .

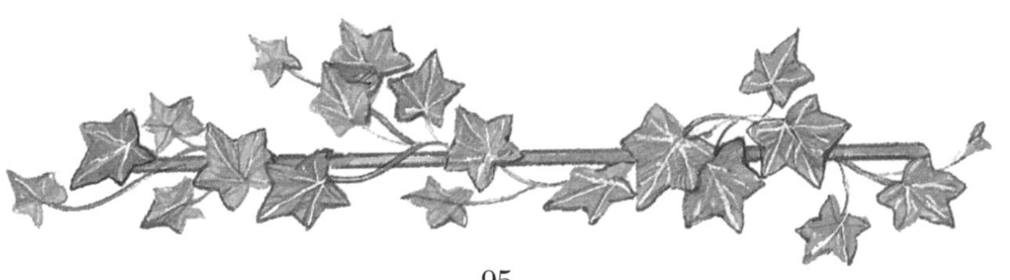

The author enjoys hearing from her readers.
Letters may be addressed as follows:

B.J. Hoff
c/o Product Editors
Warner Press
P.O. Box 2499
Anderson, IN 46018